sales compensation math

Jerome A. Colletti, Mary S. Fiss & J. Mark Davis

About WorldatWork®

The Total Rewards Association

WorldatWork (www.worldatwork.org) is an association of human resource professionals from FORTUNE 500 and other leading organizations worldwide focused on attracting, motivating and retaining employees.

Founded in 1955, WorldatWork provides practitioners with training and education to effectively design and implement strategies and practices in total rewards, including compensation, benefits, work-life, recognition and career development. With offices in Scottsdale, Arizona, and Washington, D.C., WorldatWork supports its 30,000 members and professionals in 75 countries with thought leadership, publications, research and community. WorldatWork administers certification through the WorldatWork Society of Certified Professionals.

The WorldatWork group of registered marks includes: WorldatWork®, workspan®, Certified Compensation Professional or CCP®, Certified Benefits Professional® or CBP, Global Remuneration Professional or GRP®, Work-Life Certified Professional or WLCP®, WorldatWork Society of Certified Professionals®, and Alliance for Work-Life Progress® or AWLP®.

WorldatWork Journal, WorldatWork Press and Telework Advisory Group are part of the WorldatWork family.

www.worldatwork.org

ISBN 978-1-57963-186-4 (Paperback/softback)
978-1-57963-2540 (E-book)

Editors: Andrea Ozias, Christina Fuoco-Karasinski

Cover Design: Melissa Neubauer

Design: Linh La

Creative Services Manager: Rebecca Williams

Table of Contents

Introduction

The mathematical ways in which the incentive pay opportunity relates to performance is a challenge common to all sales compensation plan designers. How an incentive formula—bonus, commission or a combination—is developed involves correctly applying mathematics to achieve a company's desired pay-for-performance goal among the salesforce. Regardless of the strategic direction intended by the plan, if the math associated with the formula is flawed, the plan will not work as intended. Also, if the formula used to calculate incentive pay is too complex, the motivational value of the plan could be less than optimal. In either case, this means a company will not realize the desired behavior and performance from its investment in sales incentive pay.

Sales Compensation Math is a response to HR managers and compensation generalists who have expressed an interest in knowing how to construct the sales incentive pay formula within the context of a plan design process. Each year, a significant number of WorldatWork members enroll in the two-day certification course, "Elements of Sales Compensation." We have observed that the majority of students want to gain foundational knowledge in sales compensation plan design and implementation. Many of these students have emphasized the importance of understanding how to build sales incentive formulas because they know they will be called upon to help with that aspect of plan design at some point.

This book is written to provide the HR manager and compensation generalist with a reference guide that places relevant information about formula design and related plan mechanics in one book that is useful and easily referenced. We believe this book will serve as an effective "refresher" on the do's and don'ts of formula design for experienced compensation professionals—particularly sales compensation managers and analysts—as well as those in a sales operation role who either have full responsibility for sales compensation or spend significant time each year involved with plan design.

How This Book Can Help You

This book is designed as a companion guide to *Sales Compensation Essentials: A Field Guide for the HR Professional*, published in 2006 by WorldatWork. Essentially, *Sales Compensation Math* builds upon and significantly expands the content provided in Chapter 6 of *Sales Compensation Essentials*, "Designing a New Sales Compensation Plan."

Sales Compensation Math is organized and written to provide a "drill down" into the details of plan formula design so it can be used in several ways:

- As a reference guide to definitions, practices and techniques frequently associated with an incentive formula that HR professionals and compensation practitioners need to be aware of when developing plans. It will help you acquire the knowledge and master the use of terms that you will need to help top managers—particularly sales executives and financial officers—make informed choices about the most appropriate incentive formula to adopt in a plan.
- As a "how-to" guide that developers of sales compensation plans can use when constructing the formula associated with the appropriate incentive design.
- As an authoritative source of illustrations and examples of various mathematical applications—basic and advanced techniques—that are associated with sales incentive pay, including commission and bonus formulas.

How This Book Is Organized

Sales Compensation Math is organized into five chapters. Each chapter corresponds to the way in which most HR professionals or compensation generalists face the challenges of sales incentive formula design. Chapter 1, "Cash Building Blocks," sets the stage for incentive formula design by briefly identifying, defining and illustrating terms that will be influenced by mathematical applications. This is largely a review and summary of material that has been used in *Sales Compensation Essentials*, and thus can either stand alone or provide an easy transition as the foundation required for this book.

Chapter 2, "Performance Measurement and Payout," describes practices and techniques that are essential to incentive formula design regardless of the plan type used—commission or bonus. Approaches to goal setting, establishing the performance range, setting weights for performance measures, quota credit alternatives and implications, and determining the right payout period (cumulative versus discrete) are design challenges that must be appropriately addressed before applying math to formula design.

Chapter 3, "Commissions," and Chapter 4, "Bonuses," are the heart of this book.

They provide details about how to apply math to incentive formula design. Each type of commission and bonus is discussed in detail relative to three topics:

- Its definition and typical use
- The type of data or information required for the calculation
- How to do the calculation (the math associated with it).

Each chapter concludes with a description of how to finalize the formula's math.

Chapter 5, "Advanced Incentive Techniques," describes and illustrates designs involving math that are a bit more complex, and thus require careful consideration when structuring the incentive formula. Here, we explain the math required to use a commission and bonus in the same plan, how to construct a linked incentive plan and, finally, examples of various special incentive techniques designed to fit specific needs (e.g., new account bonuses, new product launch commissions, fast-start bonuses and consistency bonuses).

The definitions, techniques and step-by-step calculation methods we describe in this book can help you enhance your skills in the area of sales incentive formula design. We in no way suggest that math associated with incentive formula design supersedes other aspects of sales compensation design (e.g., sales strategy definition, job clarity, performance measures, and terms and conditions). However, it has been our experience that HR professionals and compensation generalists often do not have complete command of the fundamental math concepts and principles required to help sales executives align pay with performance through the incentive formula. We believe this is where this book is valuable. It provides the essential math tools and techniques required to construct correct and appropriate sales incentive plan formulas. Thus, the benefit we hope you gain from this book is the confidence to apply math to sales compensation to increase the effectiveness of those plans in your company.

Chapter 1
Cash Building Blocks

There are several different elements involved in establishing the target cash compensation (TCC) structure for a sales compensation plan, including setting target cash compensation levels, aging survey data, learning how mix and leverage work together and using draws. What follows in this chapter lays the foundation for incentive formula design as discussed throughout this book.

Establishing Target Cash Compensation (TCC)

TCC is the annual cash compensation amount paid for achieving expected levels of performance (e.g., 100 percent of quota), and it reflects the economic value of a job. TCC is comprised of two components:

- Base salary (a uniform salary or the midpoint of the salary range), and/or
- The target incentive compensation earned for achieving target performance on all goals or quotas.

While base salary and incentive compensation typically are used, the TCC for a "100-percent commission job" includes only the target incentive component.

There are a number of potential inputs to establishing an appropriate TCC amount, including:

- **Company Compensation Philosophy.** The company's philosophy, as well as the stated business strategy and HR goals, are foundational inputs. What is the company's desired pay position relative to market? Fiftieth percentile? Seventy-fifth percentile? Other? If the organization doesn't have an established pay philosophy, the default position often used is the 50th-percentile data from survey data. If you deviate (and any deviation typically is upward) from the 50th percentile, be ready to justify why your company needs to pay above-market TCC levels, either for all jobs or for select jobs. Are there aggressive hiring goals in place? Has the strategy changed? Have jobs changed? Is the labor pool scarce for a particular job or jobs?

- **Current and Past TCC Levels**. Along with the current TCC level of a job, be sure to consider the historical context, as well. How long has the current TCC been in place? How much has it increased in the past few years?
- **TCC Levels of Other Jobs.** Examine TCC levels for other like jobs, as well as jobs that are at a higher and lower level than the job in question. For example, when setting the TCC for an Account Executive role in a particular business unit, look at comparable selling roles in other business units. Also, consider higher- and lower-level jobs to help with internal leveling (e.g., a National Account Manager as a higher-level job and a Sales Representative as a lower level job).
- **Recruiting Insights.** Understanding the current realities of the labor market can be helpful in establishing a competitive TCC level. This should include input from front-line sales managers and recruiters typically used by your company. However, beware of the tendency to inflate a recruiting candidate's current TCC or the actual total cash compensation earned, and use measures to validate these data where possible. Getting a candidate's sales quota level in addition to the TCC amount is one way to do this. Another is to "discount" this type of input by up to 25 percent, as recruiters typically provide information on "top" or 90th-percentile candidates.
- **Exit-Interview Results.** Exit interviews with salespeople who voluntarily terminate employment can yield helpful insights on a number of sales management dimensions, including sales compensation. It is especially useful to get information about the TCC level they have signed on for in their new job.
- **External Survey Data.** Survey data tends to be viewed as the "Holy Grail" in terms of establishing TCC levels. However, this is only one of many inputs to consider. Where possible, avoid using external data as the exclusive input into establishing TCC levels.

  Survey data are only as good as the extent to which the survey jobs match the jobs you are attempting to market price. Unfortunately, most pay surveys provide only minimal descriptions of benchmark jobs, making the task of job matching difficult.

  Where possible, use more than one job match and calculate the average value from the two or three data points. Job-matching sessions hosted by the company conducting the survey also are useful in confirming the degree to which your job is a "match." Depending on the strength of the match, the job may need to be priced using an adjustment factor.

For example, if the survey job is deemed to be a "light" match relative to the job you are attempting to match (i.e., the survey job is at a lower level or doesn't contain all the elements of the job you are matching), then a positive adjustment factor (e.g., 10 percent) is applied to the raw TCC survey data as follows:

Raw TCC Survey Data	x	Adjusted Factor for Light Match	=	Adjusted Raw Survey Data
$82,500		110%		$90,750

Conversely, if the survey match is a "heavy" match (i.e., bigger than the job you are attempting to match), then a negative adjustment factor or discount is applied to the raw survey data. The following is an example that discounts the survey data by 10 percent:

Raw TCC Survey Data	x	Adjustment Factor for Heavy Match	=	Adjusted Raw Survey Data
$82,500		90%		$74,250

Aging Survey Data

The effective date of survey data stated in the survey report typically lags the intended effective date for the implementation of the new target pay levels. As such, when market pricing sales jobs, the survey data need to be "aged" forward to match the date on which you intend the new pay levels to take effect. This often coincides with the effective date for a new sales compensation plan.

For example, if your fiscal year and planned launch of a new sales compensation plan both begin on Jan. 1, and the survey effective date is Aug. 1, then the data needs to be aged forward from the Aug. 1 values to be current as of the new plan effective date on Jan. 1.

Aging Formula Inputs

The formula for aging survey data requires only two inputs:

- The number of months the data needs to be aged, and
- The annual growth rate with which you want to age the data.

The first input simply is a function of the number of months between the survey effective date and the date to which you want to age the data to make it current. Using the preceding example, survey data effective Aug. 1 must be aged a total of five months to be current as of Jan. 1. The second input, the annual growth rate, can be a reflection of a number of factors, including:

- Your company's overall planned merit increase budget

- The anticipated annual base pay and/or total compensation growth percentage in a given industry
- A broad, external projection of base pay growth, such as the projection provided each year by WorldatWork in its annual *Salary Budget Survey* report and updates.

Aging Formula: The Mechanics

The formula for calculating the aging factor to be used on raw survey data one year older or less, using the two inputs explained above, is as follows:

$$1 + (x*n/12)$$

In this formula, "x" is the annual growth rate and "n" is the number of months the data need to be aged. This is simply the pro rata portion of the annual growth rate ("x"), based on the number of months the data need to be aged ("n").

To illustrate the aging formula, assume our inputs are:

- Survey effective date of Aug. 1 and new plan effective date of Jan. 1 (five months later)
- Annual growth rate of 3.5 percent.

With these inputs, the aging factor would be calculated as follows:

$$1 + (.035*5/12) = \text{Aging Factor}$$
$$1 + 0.0146 = 1.0146$$

The aging factor to be applied to the survey data in this example is 1.0146.

Applying the Aging Factor

To apply the aging factor, simply multiply the raw survey data by the aging factor. For example, assuming the raw data from your Aug. 1 survey job match suggests a TCC amount of $82,500, and using the aging factor calculated above, the aged or updated market data would be calculated as follows:

Raw Survey Data (as of Aug. 1)		Aging Factor		Aged Survey Data (as of Jan. 1)
$82,500	x	1.0146	=	$83,703

In this example, $83,703 is the "aged" or current market value for the job from the survey as of the new plan effective date of Jan. 1. This aged survey data result, along with the other inputs described in the previous section, would be factored into the process of establishing TCC levels.

Salary/Incentive Ratio

The salary/incentive ratio, often referred to as the "mix," is the relationship between the base salary (either the uniform salary or the midpoint of the salary range) and the target incentive compensation amount in the TCC package at planned or expected performance. The two portions of the pay mix, expressed as percentages, always sum to 100 percent. For example, a 70/30 pay mix means that 70 percent of the TCC for the job is in base salary (either the uniform salary for the job or the salary range midpoint), and 30 percent is in target incentive compensation.

There are a number of factors to consider in determining the most appropriate pay mix for a job. However, the primary driver of pay mix is a job's relative degree of influence on the customer's buy decision relative to all of the other variables in the marketing mix (e.g., brand awareness, pricing, product quality, advertising and promotion, etc.). More information on the factors to consider in determining mix can be found in Chapters 2 and 6 of the book *Sales Compensation Essentials*.

Using Mix to Calculate the Target Compensation Structure

Once the desired pay mix is determined, calculate the base salary or salary range midpoint and the target incentive by applying the mix percentages to the TCC level for a job, as illustrated in the following example:

- TCC: $120,000
- Mix: 60/40

TCC $120,000	x	Base Salary Portion of Mix 60%	=	Base Salary or Salary Midpoint $72,000
TCC $120,000	x	Target Incentive Portion of Mix 40%	=	Target Incentive Compensation $48,000

In this example, the $120,000 TCC with a 60/40 pay mix results in a base salary of $72,000 and a target incentive of $48,000.

Calculating the Incentive Opportunity

Once the structure of the TCC is determined, there are several ways to calculate the incentive opportunity (as described in Chapter 2 of *Sales Compensation Essentials*). The most appropriate method is based on the company's pay philosophy.

If the goal is to provide a uniform mix for each individual within a job (i.e., each person has the same proportion of pay at risk), two approaches will achieve that goal:

- A uniform salary is paid to all incumbents within a job (e.g., using the above TCC example, all Sales Representatives are paid a salary of $72,000 per year, regardless of tenure, experience or performance), and a uniform incentive opportunity (e.g., $48,000, using the above example) also is provided.
- A uniform *percent of salary* is applied to the base pay of each individual to calculate the incentive opportunity for that individual. The formula for calculating the percent of base as the incentive opportunity is:

$$\frac{\text{Target Incentive Proportion of TCC}}{\text{Base Proportion of TCC}} = \text{Target Incentive as Percent of Base}$$

Figure 1-1 provides several examples of the results of this formula.

If the goal is to ensure that the mix applies to the job—not the individual—then a uniform incentive opportunity is calculated based on the target mix. As illustrated in Figure 1-2, that results in a more aggressive actual mix for those individuals lower in the salary range, in this case 56/44, and a less aggressive mix for those higher in the range, in this case 64/36.

Figure 1-1

Target Incentive as a Percent of Base

Mix	Percent of Base
90/10	11%
80/20	25%
75/25	33%
60/40	67%
50/50	100%

Figure 1-2

Mix Varies by Individual Salary

Mix	60/40
Salary Range	$60,000-$84,000
Midpoint	$72,000
Target Incentive	$48,000

Salary	Target Incentive	Mix
$60,000	$48,000	56%/44%
$72,000	$48,000	60%/40%
$84,000	$48,000	64%/36%

Leverage

Leverage is defined as the upside incentive opportunity earned for above-target performance. Specifically, leverage is the amount of incremental incentive compensation available for performance at a defined level above target or quota, often referred to as the "excellence" performance level. Excellence performance typically is modeled to reflect the anticipated 90th percentile performance level. In other words, only 1 in 10 salespeople in a given role is expected to achieve or exceed the excellence performance level. It is at "excellence" that the full amount of upside leverage is earned (see Chapter 2 for more on establishing the excellence level in the performance range). Finally, a defined leverage does not require a plan cap, but rather determines the slope of the payout curve (or "payout line") associated with performance.

How Leverage Is Expressed

Leverage often is expressed either as a ratio of the upside leverage to the target incentive (e.g., a 2:1 leverage ratio), or as a multiple of the target incentive amount (e.g., a 3x leverage multiple). In either case, the incumbent has the opportunity to earn an incremental two times the target incentive (2:1 ratio), or a total incentive compensation level of three times the target incentive amount (3x multiple) for performance at excellence.

The leverage in sales compensation plans often ranges from as low as a 1:1 ratio or 2x leverage multiple to the aforementioned 2:1 or 3x leverage multiple. The amount of leverage in a plan depends largely on a job's prominence, the amount of pay at risk in the mix and plan affordability. There are a number of resources available to help determine the appropriate amount of upside leverage to build into a sales compensation plan, as described in Chapters 2 and 6 of *Sales Compensation Essentials*.

Calculating Leverage

To calculate the leverage of a sales compensation plan using the leverage multiple approach and the assumptions listed below, simply apply the leverage multiple to the job's target incentive amount as follows:

- TCC: $120,000
- Mix: 60/40
- Target Incentive: $48,000 ($120,000 TCC x 40% target incentive portion of the mix)
- Leverage multiple: 3.0

Target Incentive $48,000	x	Leverage Multiple 3.0	=	Total Incentive Earned at "Excellence" $144,000

In this example, an incremental $96,000 ($144,000-$48,000) of incentive compensation is earned for above-target performance, resulting in a total incentive payout of $144,000 at the excellence performance level. Placing the upside average in the context of the definition of excellence performance allows one to model the slope of the payout curve above target. **When developing the slope of the payout curve, it is critical to use the right formulas and review the results to guard against either "over" or "under" paying based on performance and financial viability.** See Chapters 3 and 4 for more information on modeling the slope of the payout curve to depict upside leverage in the context of a commission and a bonus, respectively.

Mix and Leverage Working Together

Pay mix and leverage work together to create the total incentive opportunity of a given plan. There typically is a direct correlation between the amount of pay at risk in the mix (i.e., the incentive compensation tied to performance) and the amount of upside leverage. For example, a job with an aggressive mix of 40/60 often will have an equally aggressive leverage (e.g., a 2:1 ratio or 3x leverage multiple or more) to compensate for the amount of risk being carried in the plan. The reverse also is true in that a job that warrants an 85/15 mix likely will have a less aggressive leverage opportunity, such as a 1:1 ratio or 2x leverage multiple. Figure 1-3 illustrates the relationship of mix and leverage in three different scenarios.

Figure 1-3
Mix and Leverage

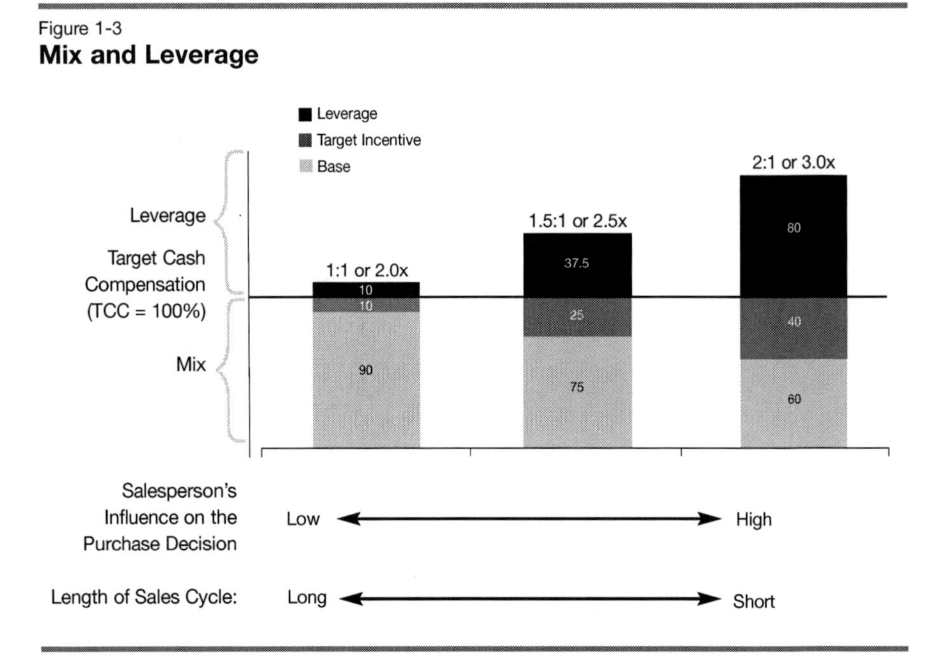

Using Draws

A draw is defined as a compensation payment provided in advance of performance. There are two types of draws: recoverable and nonrecoverable. A nonrecoverable draw acts as a "guarantee" and may be used in uncertain economic times as both a recruiting and retention tool. On the other hand, a recoverable draw is most frequently used when there is a significant proportion of pay at risk, but a fair degree of certainty that incentive earnings will meet or exceed the draw within the draw period. With both types, if performance produces incentive earnings in excess of the draw, then the salesperson receives the additional incentive compensation beyond the draw amount.

If performance produces incentive earnings that are less than a recoverable draw amount, then the salesperson must return the unearned draw (the difference between the draw and the actual earned incentive). Alternatively, the unearned draw amount may be carried forward to the next performance period. However, with a nonrecoverable draw, if the incentive earnings do not exceed the draw amount, then the unearned amount is not returned or carried forward; the salesperson keeps the full draw amount.

Two scenarios are illustrated in Figure 1-4: one in which the earned incentive is below the monthly draw, and one in which the earned incentive exceeds the monthly draw amount. It is only under the recoverable draw in Scenario 1 that a negative carryforward is incurred, thus the earned incentive is less than the draw amount.

Common Uses of Draws

In some sales jobs, the frequency of incentive earnings and payment may make it difficult for a salesperson to meet personal cash-flow requirements. A draw is an effective technique to help salespeople bridge the time between earning incentive

Figure 1-4
Draw Illustrations

	Scenario 1: Earned Incentive < Draw		Scenario 2: Earned Incentive > Draw	
Compensation Element	Recoverable	Nonrecoverable	Recoverable	Nonrecoverable
Earned incentive	$4,250	$4,250	$6,100	$6,100
Monthly draw	$5,000	$5,000	$5,000	$5,000
Net incentive/draw earned	$4,250	$5,000	$6,100	$6,100
Additional earned incentive	$0	$0	$1,100	$1,100
Negative carryforward	-$750	$0	$0	$0

pay and meeting their financial obligations. A draw is particularly valuable to salespeople if there is no base salary, or if base salary is a low proportion of TCC. There are at least three major benefits to making a draw available to salespeople:

- It does not compromise the integrity of the mix element (e.g., low or no salary/high incentive) in the sales compensation plan
- It continues to emphasize performance
- It provides cash flow so that salespeople can focus on the appropriate behavior that drives results.

When a draw is used to help bridge incentive compensation earnings for new-hire salespeople, it typically is offered for a limited term to allow the new employee to progress up the learning curve far enough to be at least moderately self sufficient from an incentive earnings standpoint. The length of the draw term varies on the following factors:

- The amount of time expected for the salesperson to become fairly proficient in the job
- The length of the sales cycle
- The incentive payout frequency built into the plan
- The affordability of the draw, particularly if nonrecoverable.

Draw terms of three to six months are fairly common for new-hire salespeople, while draw terms of more than 12 months are rare.

In addition to using a draw to bridge incentive earnings for new salespeople, draws also are used as a form of ongoing fixed compensation in lieu of a base salary. For example, for jobs that are "100 percent commission" (i.e., there is no base salary offered as part of the job's compensation), then a draw may be used constructively to provide compensation that the salesperson can depend on each week or month. Again, the type of draw used can be either recoverable or nonrecoverable. In this context, there is no limited time period or term after which the draw program expires. The draw is an ongoing part of the sales compensation plan.

Calculating Draws

The first step in using a draw is to determine the type of draw to use: recoverable versus nonrecoverable. Key factors, as noted earlier, include the current economic environment, the financial viability of a draw, the proportion of pay at risk and job factors (e.g., length of the sales cycle). With that decision made, the next step is to determine the amount of the draw to be paid each period. The amount of the draw often is determined as a percentage of the target incentive and typically is established at or below 100 percent of the target incentive amount.

One approach is to set the draw amount as a percent of the target incentive based on consistent prior performance. For example, if a sales representative's performance is 90 percent or greater of goal over a defined number of prior performance periods, he/she may be entitled to "draw" 75 percent of the target incentive. Alternatively, a sales representative who performs in a range of 70 percent to 89 percent of goal may only be entitled to "draw" 35 percent of the target incentive. And a sales representative who performs below 70 percent of goal may not be entitled to any draw against the target incentive.

Summing Up

Constructing an appropriate cash compensation opportunity is the foundation of effective sales compensation plan design. It is the cash incentive compensation opportunity that is then delivered to a salesperson on the basis of performance in any number of the incentive forms and mechanics described in Chapters 3 through 5 of this book. While there are many considerations in designing an effective incentive formula for a given role or business context, getting the cash compensation opportunity right is an important first step.

Chapter 2
Performance Measurement and Payout

The effectiveness of a sales incentive compensation plan—commission or bonus—relies heavily on how goals (or quotas) are assigned, the value placed on achieving those goals and the performance period applied to payout under the plan. There are elements of math that apply to these topics, and they are independent of the sales incentive pay formula. It is useful to understand what and how various forms of math apply to these topics before discussing commission and bonus calculations.

Approaches to Assigning Sales Goals

Goals flow from a company's business mission and cascade through the organization to communicate the specific performance objectives a company desires its functions, teams or individual employees to achieve. To the salesforce, these goals focus each individual on the specific performance that determines his/her financial, as well as nonfinancial, rewards. The first step in assigning goals to the salesforce is to consider the types of goals that must be set in the context of a current sales incentive compensation plan. Essentially, there are two types of goals:

- Quantitative goals focus on what or how much salespeople are expected to achieve.
- Qualitative goals reflect either expectations about how salespeople achieve quantitative goals (from a behavioral or process perspective) or critical milestones or projects that lead to an economic result.

Calculating Quantitative Goals

Companies use three basic processes to calculate and assign quantitative goals to salespeople, resulting in "major account goals," "fair-share sales goals" and "algorithmic sales goals." The sales situation—markets, products and the role of salespeople doing business with customers within those markets—largely determines which of the three processes a company uses to calculate and assign sales goals.

Major Account Goals

Definition and Typical Use

Account planning is the most common process used to arrive at sales performance goals for sales situations in which a territory is defined as a limited number of accounts and customer-specific business development plans define the main selling activities and outcomes. This approach is used because, for a limited set of customers, it is possible to readily gather and use the following data and information:

- Past sales/share of business and account-growth potential
- Purchasing practices
- Products/services application to a particular customer's needs.

How to Determine Major Account Goals Using Account Planning

Figure 2-1 illustrates the results of using account planning to arrive at an initial total sales growth for a single territory (in this case, named customers and target accounts). This process requires that an Account Executive assemble a database and make judgments and calculations as follows:

- Identifies all customers and target accounts in the territory (Column 1)
- Estimates the account total sales potential for the company's product as a basis for determining how much growth is possible with the account (Column 2)

Figure 2-1

Calculating Major Account Goals Using Account Planning Process

1	2	3	4	5	6	7
Customer or Target Account	Estimated Account Sales Potential	Prior 12-Month Actual Sales	Joint AE/Customer Planning Incremental Sales Estimate	Estimated Probability for New Sales	Estimated New Sales	Initial Sales Goal
Customer 1	$2,000,000	$500,000	$50,000	50%	$25,000	$525,000
Customer 2	$4,000,000	$500,000	$20,000	75%	$15,000	$215,000
Customer 3	$6,000,000	$500,000	-	0%	-	$600,000
Target A	$1,000,000	-	$100,000	25%	$25,000	$25,000
Target B	$5,000,000	-	$50,000	75%	$37,500	$37,500
Target C	$2,000,000	-	$30,000	75%	$22,500	$22,500
Total	$20,000,000	$1,300,000	$250,000		$125,000	$1,425,000
					Growth %	9.6%
					Company's Target Growth Goal	12%
					Difference	2.4%

- Assembles prior 12-month actual sales (Column 3)
- Estimates the potential for sales growth (e.g., increased usage, new application opportunities, taking share from competitors) based on a joint planning session with key buyers or decision makers in the accounts (Column 4)
- Estimates the probability that projected new sales will be realized (Column 5)
- Estimates new sales (dollars) based on those probabilities (Column 6)
- Calculates initial sales goal (Column 7)

In the example in Figure 2-1, the result is a forecasted increase of 9.6 percent over prior year. This is 2.4 percentage points below the company's target growth goal of 12 percent. To close this gap, an Account Executive most likely will be asked to reforecast sales to bring the level of the sales goal up to or greater than the company's expected increase.

Fair-Share Allocation

Definition and Typical Use

The fair-share allocation method assigns a company's total sales goal to each territory based on its historic percent contribution to total results in previous years. This approach is used when there are many accounts and prospects in an assigned territory and sales management believes that assigning goals based on history is appropriate because historic growth trends are expected to continue. In many cases, however, the results of the initial fair-share allocation method are modified up or down based on factors such as market volatility, competitive intensity and the salesperson's years of experience. Territories that show strong growth (overall or for particular strategic products) would be assigned a proportionately higher fair share of the company's annual goal, while territories with flat or declining sales would be allocated proportionately less of the company's goal.

How to Determine Fair-Share Allocation Goals

The calculation of fair-share goals requires at least three years of sales data for each territory (i.e., the roll-up of accounts or customers that form the territory for which the goal is being calculated). Typically, that length of time provides a reasonably large database to observe sales trends in territories. **While more than three years of data may be considered in some situations, changes in relevant accounts and customers may result in an analysis that does not account for factors such as mergers, acquisitions and significant market changes.**

For each year, a particular territory's total sales is divided by the total sales of the aggregate sale entity (e.g., company, country, division, business unit) to arrive at the territory's percent contribution. Next, the year-over-year percent growth or change in each territory's total sales is calculated. Finally, to arrive at an initial fair-share goal for an upcoming year, the percent change (from the prior two years) is applied to the most current prior year.

How this process applies to and is calculated for two illustrative sales territories over a three-year time frame is provided in Figure 2-2. Also, as explained, the initial fair-share goals can be shifted up or down based on specific factors. Figure 2-3 illustrates that process and relevant calculations.

Figure 2-2
Fair Share Goal-Setting Process

	Territory A			Territory B		
Process and Calculations	Y1	Y2	Y3	Y1	Y2	Y3
Calculate territory's percent contribution to total sales	1.0%	1.5%	2.0%	2.0%	1.7%	1.5%
Calculate percent change in year-over-year growth	-	50%	33%	-	(15%)	(12%)
Calculate upcoming year's percent change (average of Y2 and Y3) in growth rate	= 41.5%			= (13.5%)		
Calculate upcoming year's expected sales contribution (i.e., fair-share goal) using the following formula: Y3 + (Y3 x average growth rate)	2.0% + (2.0% x 41.5%) = 2.83%			1.5% + (1.5% x -13.5%) = 1.30%		

Figure 2-3
Modified Fair-Share Goals

	Territory A	Territory B
Fair-Share Goal	2.83%	1.3%
Adjust upward/downward in increments of 5% (no more than 10%) to enhance goals based on specific factors that influence a territory's potential and a salesperson's effectiveness.		
Market growth potential	0%	+ 5%
Market share	-10%	+10%
Competitive intensity	-5%	-10%
Salesperson experience in territory	+10%	-10%
Total adjustment	-5%	-5%
Modified Fair-Share Goal	2.69% (2.83% x 95%)	1.24% (1.3% x 95%)

Algorithm Allocation Method

Definition and Typical Use

The algorithm allocation method is a process that uses a statistical model to project sales and convert that projection into territory quotas. The most common statistical methods used are correlation and linear regression formula. While both methods look at the relationship between variables, the results of each type of analysis are reported differently. Figures illustrating those differences are provided later in this section. Companies with many points of purchase often use an algorithm method to make the initial assignment of goals or quotas to salespeople in their territories. This requires a company to build a database and apply a statistical model to relate one predictive variable to another for all territories for one or more prior years. This method works best in sales environments where external market data is available and the territories have, on average, 50 or more accounts.

How to Determine Sales Goals Using an Algorithm Method

When an algorithm is used to arrive at salespeople's quotas, the most common set of variable are:

Measure 1	Measure 2
Sales Dollars	Margin Dollars
Market Share Percent	Sales Increase Percent
Market Volume Growth (in dollars)	Sales Growth (in dollars)
Market Share Percent	Sales Volume (in dollars)

Typically, either correlation analyses or regression analyses—or a combination of the two—are used. Both of these analyses are available in Microsoft Excel through the Data Analysis Tool.

- **Correlation.** This type of analysis looks at pairs of variables to find out whether the two variables tend to move together either positively (as one variable grows, so does the other) or negatively (small values of one variable tend to be associated with large values of the other), or whether values of both variables tend to be unrelated. The closer the correlation is to "1" (or 100 percent), the greater the correlation. Figure 2-4 provides an illustration of a negative correlation: The value of the correlation between sales growth (x-axis) and market volume growth (y-axis) is -37 percent. While this is a fairly weak correlation, it may indicate that territories with greater market volume growth tend to have a lower sales volume growth rate.

  Figure 2-5 illustrates a positive correlation (with a correlation value of 76 percent) between two measures: market share percent (y-axis) and sales volume (x-axis). It shows that as market share increases, sales volume increases at approximately the same rate. From a sales quota assignment

Figure 2-4
Negative Correlation Illustration:
Market Volume Growth vs. Sales Growth

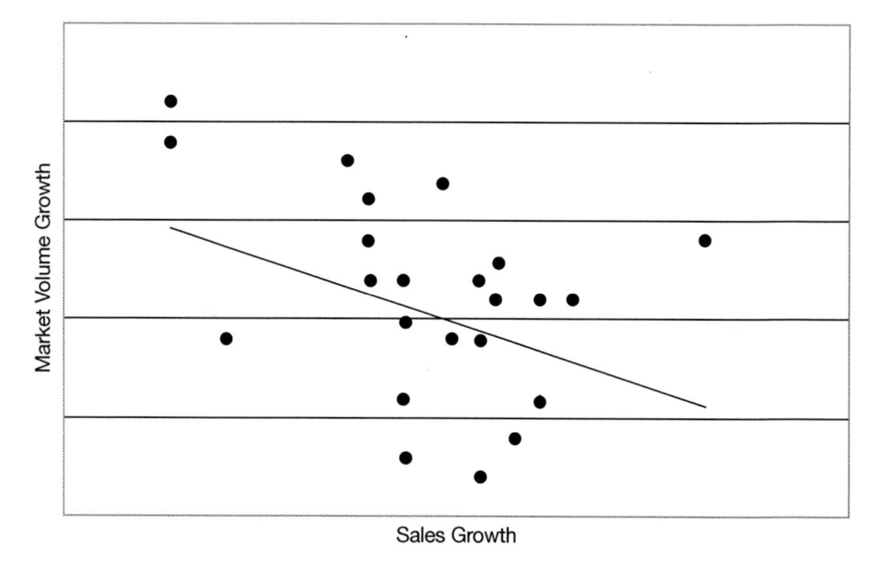

	Sales	Market Volume Growth
Sales Growth	1	
Market Volume Growth	-37%	1

perspective, this relationship suggests that territories with low market share/low sales have a much greater opportunity to grow (thus, a higher assigned sales-growth factor) than territories with high market share/sales (thus, a lower assigned sales-growth factor).

- **Linear Regression.** A regression analyzes how a single dependent variable is affected by the values of one or more independent variables. In other words, the regression analysis helps determine if one or more independent variables can predict a result or effect on a dependent variable. The regression analysis yields a correlation factor called "r squared," or R^2. The closer the R^2 value is to "1" (100 percent), the stronger the predictive relationship. (Generally speaking, a predictive value of 70 percent or more is considered a strong relationship.) To establish goals, regressions can be done to analyze how sales growth is affected by factors such as market share, market growth or previous

Figure 2-5
Positive Correlation Illustration: Market Share Percent vs. Sales Volume

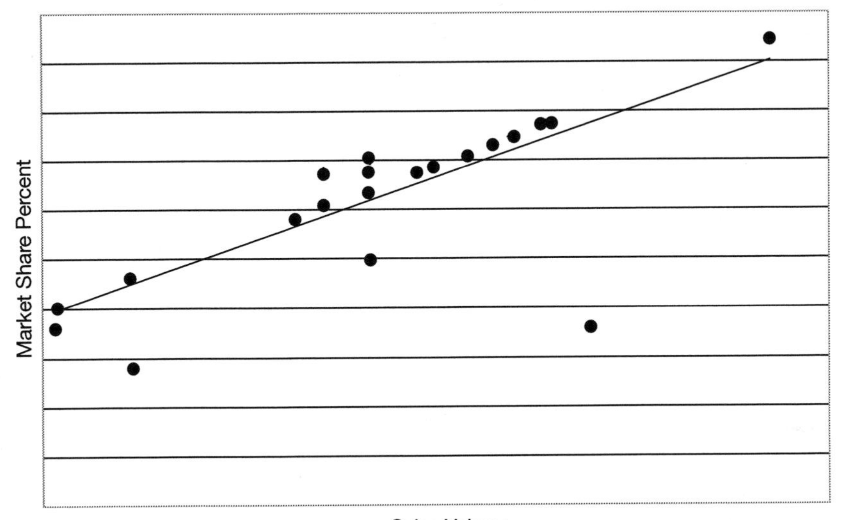

	Sales Volume	Market Share Percent
Sales	1	
Market Share	76%	1

sales. Figure 2-6 illustrates a meaningful relationship between sales and margin confirmed by an R^2 value of 72 percent—as sales volume grows, margin dollars also grow. (The dependent variable is illustrated on the y-axis.) Figure 2-7 on page 25 shows a weak relationship (R^2 is significantly below 70 percent) between sales increase and market share.

Determining Qualitative Goals

Qualitative goals differ from quantitative goals in that even though they may be measured, there often are areas of subjectivity in the evaluation. Because companies often find it useful to include qualitative goals in a sales incentive compensation plan, it is helpful to provide structure around the types of goals that are acceptable. Doing so can minimize varying and inconsistent practices in evaluating sales success relative to those goals.

There are two common categories of qualitative sales goals: Results-oriented and process-oriented.

Figure 2-6

Linear Regression Illustration: Sales vs. Margin

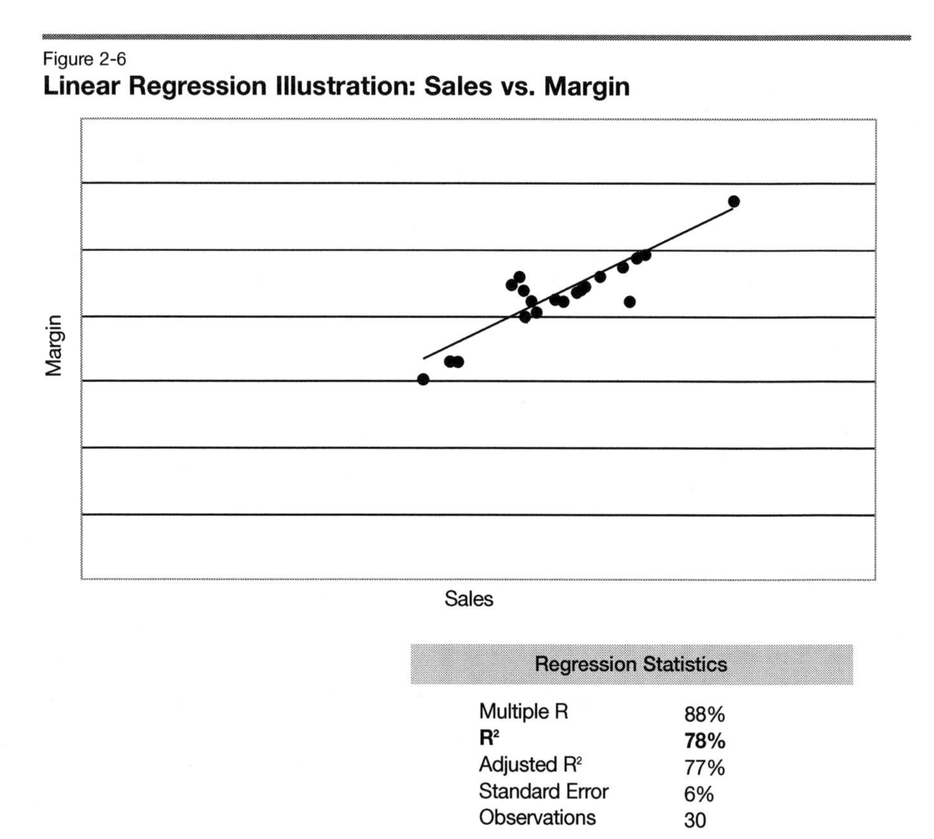

Regression Statistics	
Multiple R	88%
R^2	**78%**
Adjusted R^2	77%
Standard Error	6%
Observations	30

Results-Oriented Qualitative Goals

Definition and Typical Use

Results-oriented qualitative goals contribute to or enhance one or more of the quantitative sales performance measures. These goals commonly are used in situations in which there is a strong relationship between a particular type of sales effort or activity and sales outcomes (e.g., incremental revenue, increased account share).

How to Determine Results-Oriented Qualitative Goals

Determining the appropriate results-oriented qualitative goals to include in a sales incentive plan requires a judgment on the part of sales leadership about effort or activities that are closely related to sales success as measured by quantitative goals. Common examples of results-oriented qualitative goals include:

- Account penetration goals (e.g., movement from "x percent" to "y percent" share of the account; displacement of one or more current competitive suppliers)
- Achievement of a design win for a particular strategically important product
- Achievement of a key account milestone, (e.g., implementation of a new

Figure 2-7

Linear Regression Illustration: Market Share vs. Sales Increase

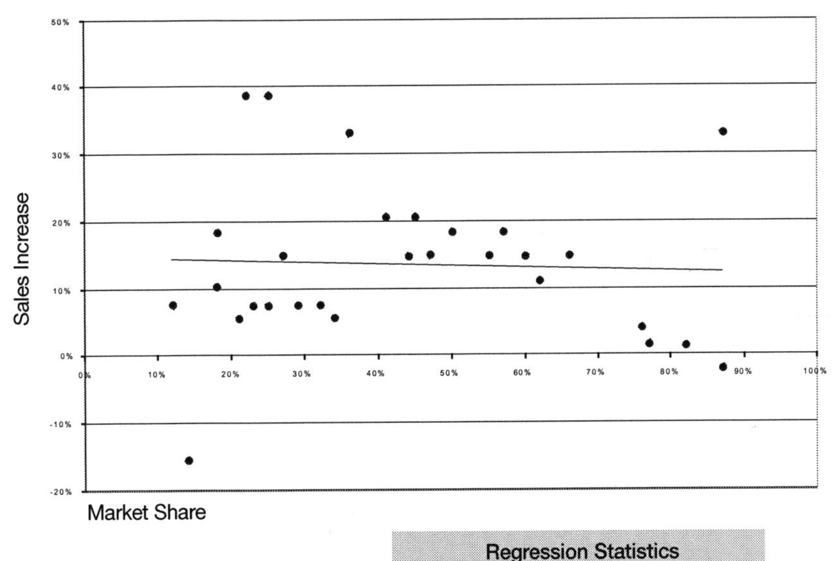

Regression Statistics	
R^2	44%
Observation (data points)	30

manufacturing line that uses the company's products as a component, or achievement of formulary status for a prescription medication).

Process-Oriented Qualitative Goals

Definition and Typical Use

Process-oriented qualitative goals contribute to or enhance the company's business relationship with customers. These goals commonly are used in situations in which a company is emphasizing new skills and competencies required to execute added or changed responsibilities to one or more of its sales jobs.

How to Determine Process-Oriented Qualitative Goals

Like results-oriented qualitative goals, the assignment of process goals is largely based on sales leadership judgment about the type of effort or activity required in advance of desired quantitative sales results. Common examples of process goals that companies use include:

- Partnering with a strategic customer on new product development
- Customized service agreements
- Win-back strategy/plan for prior year's lost business
- Contract management improvements (e.g., percent of contracts in compliance with terms and conditions, volume commitments).

Establishing the Performance Range

In most companies, sales performance is not a single result (e.g., achieving 100 percent of quota), but rather a range of results. That range—typically referred to as the performance range—is bounded by minimum performance and outstanding performance. "Threshold" is the term most commonly used to refer to the minimum level an employee must achieve before the company pays sales incentive compensation. "Excellence" is the term most commonly used to refer to outstanding performance, and it reflects the anticipated 90th percentile of all individuals whose performance is measured.

How to Determine the Performance Range

Figure 2-8 illustrates a performance distribution involving two variables: quota (x-axis) and number of territories (y-axis). Because quota is a known variable, the challenge in arriving at an appropriate performance range is to solve for threshold (X) and excellence (Y) performance points. Rules of thumb serve a useful purpose in solving for both of those performance points because there is no one common formula that applies in all situations.

To arrive at the threshold (X) point in Figure 2-8, the process is:

- **Step 1:** Calculate the ratio of prior-year actual sales to the current year's quota to arrive at an initial threshold value.

  Rule of thumb: Most companies will not set the threshold point below prior-year actual sales. For example, if $100 million was achieved last year and that equaled 95 percent of plan, what percent of this year's plan is $100 million? If it equals 90 percent of this year's plan, that would be the initial threshold value.

- **Step 2:** Determine if prior-year actual sales is an acceptable threshold point to management; if not, by what factor should that initial threshold level be increased?

  Rule of thumb: If a year-over-year price increase is implemented, it is common practice to build 50 percent of the price increase into the threshold performance. For example, based on the above, if a price increase of 10 percent is implemented, then an additional 5 percent is built into the threshold. The threshold would then be 90 percent + 5 percent, or 95 percent.

- **Step 3:** Test for the percent of the salesforce that could reasonably be expected to achieve quota based on the prior two years' performance.

  Rule of thumb: 90 percent of the sales territories (salesforce) should achieve threshold performance. For our examples, this means that 90 percent of the

Figure 2-8
Setting the Performance Range

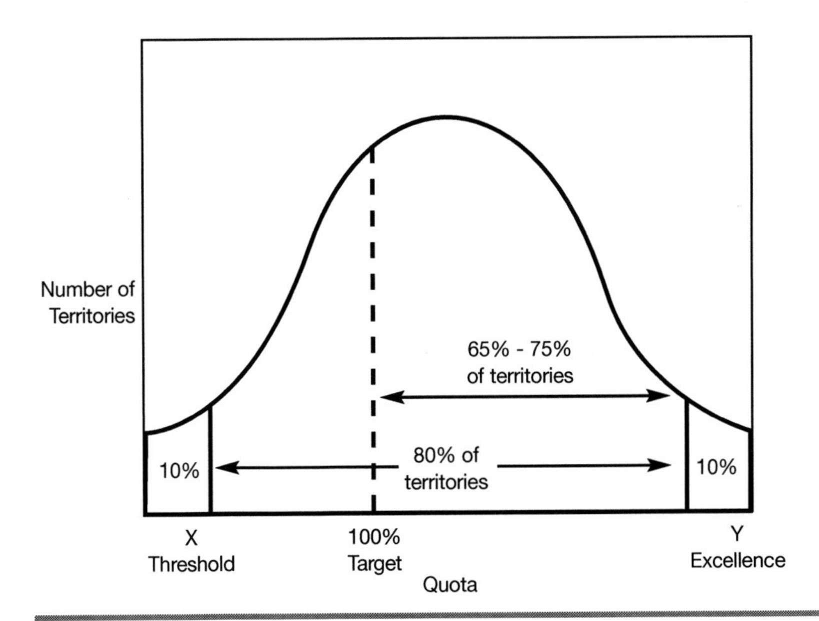

salesforce would achieve 95 percent of quota or greater over the prior two years. If significantly less than 90 percent have been below a 95-percent threshold over the past two years, the process should consider a realistically lower threshold.

To arrive at the excellence (Y) performance level in Figure 2-8, the process is as follows:

- **Step 1:** Based on historical sales results (two or more prior years), identify the actual performance level (as percent to quota) of the top 10 percent of the salesforce (i.e., the 90th percentile quota achievement level).
- **Step 2:** Relate the historical performance achievement to the new year's quota to arrive at excellence performance level.
- **Step 3:** Test for the size of payout that would be made to a salesperson at the excellence performance level

  Rule of thumb: It should be financially worthwhile for a salesperson to over-achieve, typically another 50 percent of the target incentive, or greater.

Performance-Measure Weighting

It is common practice for the sales incentive plan to include more than one performance measure. When that is the case, the weight given to each performance measure indicates how much achievement of the performance measure's target is worth relative to the entire target incentive opportunity. The objective of assigning varying performance weights is to communicate to sales personnel the relative importance of the desired sales results: The higher the weight, the more important the measure.

How to Calculate Incentive Weights

Several guidelines apply to arrive at the appropriate weight to assign to a plan's performance measures:

- No more than three measures should be used in the incentive plan.
- No measure should have less weight than 10 percent; any less means that achieving performance relative to that measure results in an insignificant amount of financial reward, and thus is less likely to be motivational.
- The highest weight should be given to sales financial measures; that is, measures aligned with achievement of revenue growth, sales and/or profit contribution.
- No measure should be assigned a weight unless there is a system available to track and credit actual results to the salesperson(s) responsible for its achievement.
- The sum of all weights must equal 100 percent.

Figure 2-9 illustrates the application of these guidelines.

It also is possible to use a performance measure with a weight of "0," as in the case of a hurdle or multiplier mechanism. This is covered in more detail in Chapter 5, where linked formula calculations are described.

Figure 2-9

Weighting Performance Measures

Target Incentive Opportunity: $40,000

Performance Measure	Incentive Weight	Measure's Incentive Value at 100% Performance
Volume	60%	$24,000
Gross Margin	25%	$10,000
Strategic Objective	15%	$6,000

Quota Credit Alternatives

The question of sales crediting is largely a function of three variables: the timing of the credit for compensation purposes, who should get credit for a sale and how sales credit is allocated to the various participants in the sale.

From a timing perspective, there are a number of sales crediting "events" that may trigger sales credit for the calculation of incentive pay, as illustrated in Figure 2-10. The pertinent question for the timing decision is, "When should the salesperson stop working on a given sale and move on to the next opportunity?" The answer to that will guide the determination of when sales credit is granted for incentive compensation purposes.

The value of a completed sale for the purpose of the incentive pay calculation is specified in the plan's quota credit rules. Who receives credit when a sale is made is an important plan design and calculation consideration because it determines how quickly in the plan year the salesperson's quota is achieved. Also, in many sales situations,

Figure 2-10

Sales Crediting Timing

"When" (Credit Event Options)	
Prior to sale	Milestone
Booking	Order accepted by company
Shipment	Order leaves the company
Invoice	Bill sent to the customer
Installation	Product installed at customer site
Payment	Monies received from the customer
Combination	Two or more of the above options

multiple salespeople receive credit on the same dollar of sales. Thus, it is important to define and calculate "how much" and "to whom" credit is given.

There are five common approaches to allocating sales results toward quota credit.

Full Credit

When a single sales resource (e.g., field sales representative, inside telesales representative) is solely responsible for securing business with a customer, 100 percent, or full credit for the sale, is assigned to that individual.

Split Credit

When multiple resources are involved with customers to secure the business, but the relative importance of the roles is quite different, each resource would receive a portion of the credit toward quota to reflect the contribution to sales success. The credit divided among those who contributed to the sale would equal 100 percent.

Multiple Credit

When multiple resources are involved with customers to secure the business and the resources have relatively equal roles, each would receive 100-percent quota credit for the sale. In this case, the quota is duplicated, as well (i.e., multiple resources are "quotaed" on the same set of customers, resulting in the sum of the individual quotas being greater than the sum of the aggregate volume at target, and greater than the business plan at target). When using a multiple-credit approach, it is common to limit the maximum percentage of any given sale that is allocated to quota credit (e.g., no more than 200 percent of any given sale can be allocated toward quota credit).

Partial Credit

In situations in which multiple resources are involved in the sale, but management wishes to limit the quota credit of one or more of the parties on the basis of a lower perceived contribution to the sale, the partial-credit approach may be used.

For example, in sales environments in which direct and indirect (e.g., channel partner) sales resources are asked to work together to effectively meet customers' needs, the direct salespeople may be awarded partial sales credit based on sales that flow through the partners.

No Credit

Occasionally, there may be a sales event for which a company does not want to award quota credit, but will make an incentive payment.

Figure 2-11 provides examples of each of the quota credit methods.

Figure 2-11
Sales Credit Assignment Options

"How Much" Credit Assignment Options	"To Whom" Definitions
Full (100%) Credit	Credit assigned to a single person (e.g., Territory Sales Representative, Telesales Representative)
Split Credit (Totals = 100%)	Credit divided among those who contributed to the sale. For example: Territory Sales Representative 75% National Account Representative 25% Total 100%
Multiple Credit (Totals >100%)	Credit assigned to two or more sales resources in an amount greater than 100%. For example: Territory Sales Representative 100% Channel Sales Representative 100%
Partial Credit (Total < 100%)	Credit is assigned to one or more sales resources in an amount less than 100%. For example: Territory Sales Representative 35% (on all sales made through the Partner Channel)
No Credit	No credit is assigned (for the purpose of quota achievement), however, incentive may be paid. Common example: multiple year sales contract

Adjusted-Value Credit

All of the preceding crediting methods use the unit of measurement that is associated with the sale based on the crediting rules in place. When there is a desire to emphasize the strategic importance of products, accounts or both, management applies adjusted-value credit to the actual sales value of a transaction. Essentially, the incentive formula (commission or bonus) is fixed, and the value of the transaction varies as a function of its makeup. When incentive pay is calculated, the adjustment factor is applied first, and the resulting value of each transaction is used to determine sales credit. Figure 2-12 on page 32 provides an example of the concept and its application. Chapter 5 provides additional information about adjusted value incentive plans and techniques.

Figure 2-12
Adjusted Value Credit Illustration

Commission Rate: 3%

Category	Relative $ Adjustment Factor
Product A	0.5
Product B	1.2
Product C	1.8
New Accounts / Product A	1.2

Example Month: June   Total Sales: $240,000

Category	Sales Volume	x	Adjustment Factor	x	Commission Rate	=	Commission Dollars
Product A	$100,000		0.5		3%		**$1,500** ($50,000 x 3%)
Product B	$75,000		1.2		3%		**$2,700** ($90,000 x 3%)
Product C	$40,000		1.8		3%		**$2,160** ($72,000 x 3%)
New Accounts / Product A	$25,000		1.2		3%		**$900** ($30,000 x 3%)
Total Commission							**$7,260**

Payout for Performance-Period Results

The performance period is the time frame over which sales results are measured and credited toward quota achievement for the purpose of incentive pay determination. There are two common approaches to incentive payment for performance period results: discrete and cumulative. The calculation of sales incentive payment is quite different under each scenario.

How to Calculate Incentive Pay Under Discrete Performance Periods

Under this definition of the performance period, incentive compensation is earned and paid for performance on a stand-alone or discrete basis. For example, the incentive earned for performance during Q1 is paid at the end of Q1 on the basis of that quarter's performance only. The same is true for each subsequent quarter regardless of performance in the previous quarter(s) or year-to-date results. Essentially, this is the equivalent of having four separate and independent sales incentive plans.

The benefit of a discrete performance-measurement approach is its simplicity. However, it is important to note that when evaluated on a full-year basis, it is likely that the annual incentive paid will not align with the annual performance relative to quota. For example, on an annual basis under a discrete plan, it is possible for below-quota performance to result in an above-target incentive payout. This is particularly true when there are significant peaks and valleys in performance results from one period to the next, combined with steep accelerators for above-target performance.

Also, under a discrete plan it can become advantageous to the salesperson to manipulate the timing of the order stream to maximize incentive earnings. In an environment where this is possible, a cumulative performance-measurement approach may be required.

How to Calculate Incentive Pay Under Cumulative Performance Periods

Using this definition of the performance period, incentive compensation is earned and paid for performance on a period-to-date basis less payments already made. A Q3 example of the formula for a cumulative year-to-date performance calculation is:

$$\frac{(\text{Q1 actual performance} + \text{Q2 actual performance} + \text{Q3 actual performance})}{(\text{Q1 quota} + \text{Q2 quota} + \text{Q3 quota})}$$

Using this example, at the end of Q3, the salesperson's performance and earnings are considered on a cumulative basis (i.e., the target incentive amount used to calculate the incentive is the Q1 through Q3 cumulative target incentive), and previous earnings paid (e.g., Q1 + Q2 earnings) are subtracted from the cumulative calculated earnings to arrive at the Q3 incentive payout.

While measuring performance on a cumulative basis is more complex than the discrete approach, the benefit is that it always aligns incentive pay with performance on an annual basis. It is almost impossible to either overpay or underpay a salesperson relative to full-year performance under the defined incentive formula. (This assumes that other variables remain constant. For example, the allocated quota and the formula do not provide an opportunity for very high overachievement pay early in the performance period.) It also eliminates any incentive for the salesperson to arbitrarily manipulate the timing of the sale. Lastly, it can help keep the salesperson focused on his/her progress toward attainment of the full-year quota as opposed to focusing on month-to-month or quarter-to-quarter results.

Examples of cumulative and discrete plans and payout calculations are provided in Chapters 3 and 4.

Allocating the Incentive Opportunity Across Performance Periods

In addition to determining the performance period over which incentive pay will be calculated, it is necessary to determine how much of the incentive opportunity is available to be earned in a period. There are three techniques that companies use to allocate the incentive opportunity across the performance periods:

- Equally divided across the periods (e.g., each quarter has the same incentive opportunity)
- Divided across the periods, consistent with the planned amount of sales in the period (e.g., historical sales represented by each quarter)
- Divided by a factor of one greater than the defined performance periods (e.g., under a quarterly plan, the factor would be five), thereby creating the opportunity to award performance in the aggregate, as well as on a cumulative basis.

Figure 2-13 provides an illustration of each technique and the associated calculation.

Figure 2-13

Allocation of Incentive Opportunity Across Performance Periods

Annual Incentive Opportunity 100%

Option 1: Equally divided across performance periods

Q1	Q2	Q3	Q4	Total
25%	25%	25%	25%	100%

$$\text{Incentive Opportunity per Period} = \frac{\text{Annual Incentive Opportunity}}{\text{4 periods}}$$

Option 2: Divided across the periods, consistent with forecasted sales in the period

Q1	Q2	Q3	Q4	Total
18%	22%	28%	32%	100%

$$\text{Incentive Opportunity per Period} = \frac{\text{Annual Incentive Opportunity}}{\text{Percent Sales Forecasted in the Period}}$$

Option 3: Divided by a factor one greater than the defined performance period

Q1	Q2	Q3	Q4	Annual	Total
20%	20%	20%	20%	20%	100%

$$\text{Incentive Opportunity per Period} = \frac{\text{Annual Incentive Opportunity}}{\text{5 periods}}$$

Summing Up

One of the biggest factors in the success of a sales compensation plan is how performance goals are determined and assigned. Companies often use quantitative and qualitative goals in the sales incentive compensation plan. There are alternative approaches to arriving at the magnitude of the goal assigned to salespeople. The most appropriate approach to assigning goals depends on sales job responsibilities and accountabilities, the data available to use in the allocation process and the information systems available to track and report results relative to goals. Regardless of the approach, a consistent process should be followed throughout the sales organization when allocating goals. Doing so increases the likelihood that the sales incentive compensation plan will contribute to the intended business results.

Assigning goals, particularly quantitative goals, typically involves a performance range that is bounded by threshold and excellence performance points. These points should be validated annually at the beginning of a new plan year.

Achievement of performance goals also is affected by how sales credit is awarded to the salesperson or salespeople involved with winning business with customers. Sales credit rules also should be reviewed and confirmed annually.

Finally, the allocation of the sales incentive compensation opportunity during the performance period(s) directly affects salesperson behavior and performance. The technique used for allocating the incentive opportunity through the plan year should be consistent with how a company's business typically flows, thus reflecting seasonality or other factors that influence unevenness in business results.

Chapter 3
Commissions

Commission is compensation paid as a percentage of sales measured in either dollars or units. This type of pay is based on a rate that is either fixed or variable, and is paid as a direct function of a sales transaction (or the total of several transactions) measured in either dollars or units. The purpose of Chapter 3 is to identify situations in which a commission may be the most effective approach to sales incentive compensation, to describe the most prevalent forms of commission formulas and to illustrate how to correctly calculate those formulas.

When to Use Commissions

Companies use commissions for a variety of reasons. Management's objectives for the business and the type of selling performed are key considerations in the selection of a commission arrangement as the sales compensation plan (or a major component of it). Commissions most typically are used:

- In high-growth environments
- Where the focus is on generating sales volume
- With a sales process that is transaction oriented and where the seller has a high degree of personal influence on each sale
- Where there is relatively equal sales potential, or sales territories (either geographic or account set) are unassigned
- When there is insufficient data for setting realistic quotas, or target setting is not reliable.

Situations in which commissions frequently are used as the appropriate approach to compensating salespeople (in total or in part) include retail settings such as consumer electronics and jewelry, realty (sales and leasing) and financial services. Payouts typically are frequent—semimonthly or monthly.

Types of Commissions

Commission formulas range from simple to complex, as illustrated in Figure 3-1.

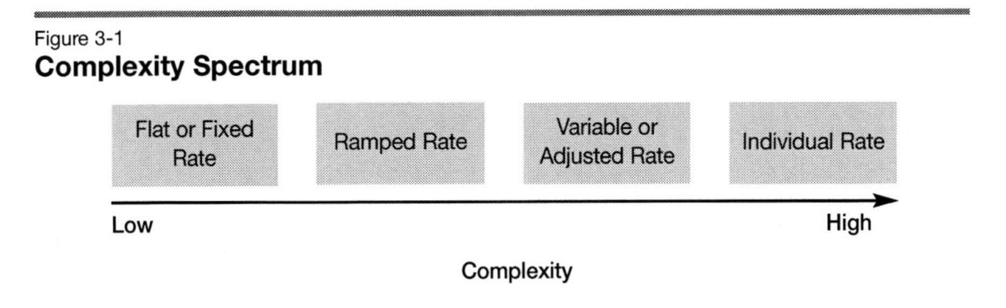

Flat or Fixed Commission

Definition and Typical Use

The rate does not vary in a fixed- or flat-rate commission approach. This is the simplest form of commission to develop and explain. A fixed rate is applied to all relevant sales to calculate the commission payout (e.g., 4 percent of sales or $100 per unit). This type of commission is most often used in new companies, companies with very small sales organizations, companies with "open" territories (territories that have no geographic boundaries) or for a new product for which there is no sales history.

How to Determine the Rate

Because the same rate applies to all sales or all units for all salespeople eligible for the commission plan, the information required to set the rate is straightforward and includes:

- The key metric that will be rewarded (e.g., revenue dollars, gross profit or margin dollars or units)
- The anticipated total volume to be achieved (either as dollars or units)
- The incentive opportunity the company offers for achievement of the anticipated total volume.

The basic formula for determining the commission rate is:

$$\frac{\text{(Number of Salespeople in Plan x Commission Incentive Opportunity)}}{\text{Total Volume Objective}}$$

Figure 3-2 provides two examples of how this formula can be applied: Where the key performance objective is revenue, and where the key objective is the number of units sold.

It is important to remember that this is one single flat rate that applies to all volume and is the same for all salespeople. If more than one rate is used, the approach will move further along the complexity spectrum to another type of commission.

How to Calculate the Payout

The calculation for determining incentive payout is simplest with a fixed- or flat-rate commission. The volume (dollars or units) is multiplied by the commission rate (percent or dollars) to determine the incentive pay earned. Each payout period typically is discrete. That is, the production for that period only is multiplied by the rate. Some examples of payout calculations are provided in Figure 3-3.

Figure 3-2
Fixed-Rate Determination Examples

Revenue Commission

Number of Sales People	20
x	
Target Incentive Opportunity	$10,000
÷	
Total Corporate Sales-Revenue Objective	$10,000,000
=	
Commission Rate	2% paid on all sales

Unit Commission

Number of Sales People	20
x	
Target Incentive Opportunity	$10,000
÷	
Total Corporate Sales Objective (Units)	1,000
=	
Commission Rate	$200 paid per unit

Ramped Commission

Definition and Typical Use

A ramped commission involves a rate change after a certain performance level, milestone or objective has been met. Ramped commission rates also are referred to as "tiered" rates. The commission rate may either increase (progressive) or

Figure 3-3
Fixed-Rate Payout Examples

Total Sales Volume		Rate		Payout
$100,000	x	2%	=	$2,000

Total Units Sold		Rate		Payout
10 units	x	$200	=	$2,000

decrease (regressive). Because rates are tied to achievement of a target performance level, a single rate typically is determined for target achievement, and different rates are provided for sales below or above target performance. "Target" may be a specified sales volume or a percent of quota achievement. Figure 3-4 shows the difference between progressive and regressive rate changes.

A ramped or "tiered" rate can be either cumulative or tied to discrete or incremental performance ranges. If the plan is discrete, then the new rate is applied only to the incremental volume associated with the new range of achievement. The calculation associated with discrete tiers is somewhat complicated because multiple steps are required. However, companies may use this approach if the value of actual performance at each tier is different, and it is not financially appropriate to pay for all performance back to threshold at the same rate.

Figure 3-4

Progressive vs. Regressive Ramp

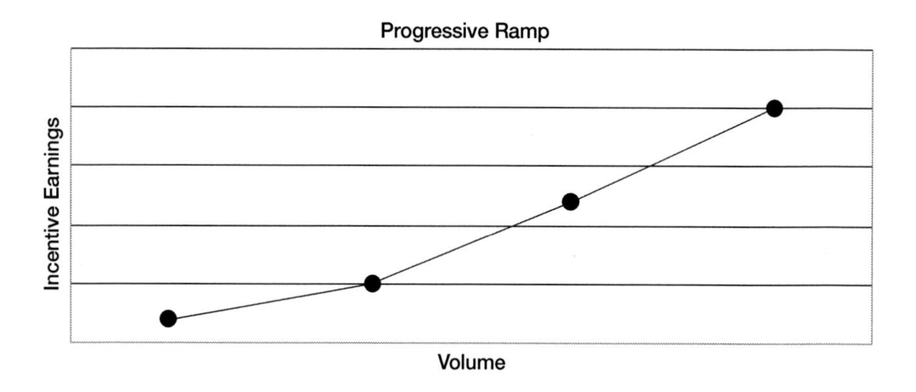

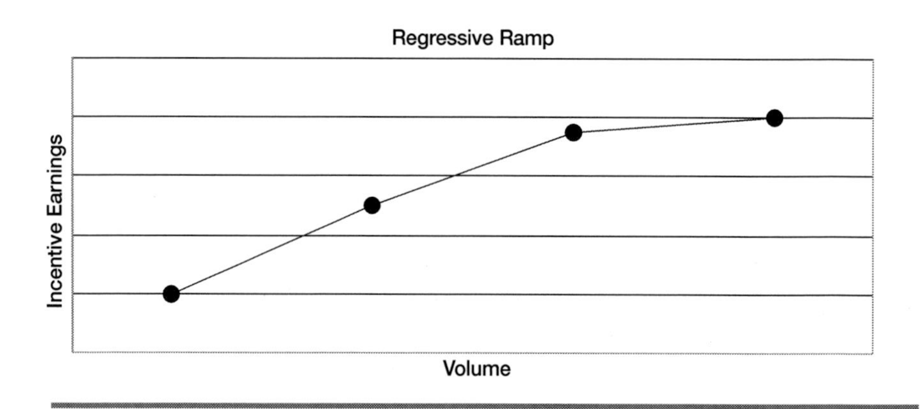

If the plan is cumulative (also known as a plan with a "lookback" or "clawback"), incentive paid versus incentive earned is recalculated at defined intervals. This approach is perceptually easier, since only one rate is applied each time the calculation is done. That is, with ascending levels of achievement, the salesperson does not need to calculate commission earnings from each tier separately. Companies may use this approach if, as achievement increases, the value of previous achievement increases.

Figure 3-5 on page 42 illustrates the difference between discrete and cumulative calculation. As you can see, if the same rate is applied, the payout for a cumulative calculation will be greater because a new rate is applied to all volume from the first dollar once a higher volume tier is achieved. Therefore, there are implications for determining the rate(s), costing the plan and communicating expectations depending on the approach used to determine the commission rates.

How to Determine the Rate

A progressive ramp might be used if:

- Each additional sale is more difficult.
- Additional sales are incrementally more profitable.
- Pay discrimination between top and marginal performance is desired.

A regressive ramp might be used if:

- Each additional sale is easier.
- The company wants to avoid windfalls (runaway earnings).
- Excessive sales are unprofitable.

To finalize the points at which the rate changes, the incremental change and, therefore, the final rates, you need:

- The key metric that will be rewarded (e.g., revenue dollars, profit or margin dollars or units)
- The anticipated total volume to be gained (either as dollars or units) at target
- The incentive opportunity the company offers for achievement of the anticipated total volume (i.e., the target incentive compensation opportunity)
- Analyses to determine at what point of achievement commissions can be paid (e.g., from first dollar or unit, or at some point of quota achievement, defined as "threshold," as explained in Chapter 2)
- Analyses to determine the financial viability of a progressive versus regressive rate plan
- Determination of whether discrete or cumulative calculation is most appropriate for the sales environment (this will be a significant factor in determining the commission rate at each level).

Figure 3-5

Discrete vs. Cumulative Formula Calculations

Quota	$1,000,000
Target Incentive Opportunity	$15,000
	Base Rate 1.5%

Percent of Quota achieved	Commission Rules
0%- 50%	0.75% (1.5% x 0.5)
50%-100%	2.25% (1.5% x 1.5)
100%-150%	3.00% (1.5% x 2)
May be capped or uncapped	

Discrete Payout Tiers	Payout for Range	Total Payout (Remember: Rate applies only to each tier. The total payouts illustrated are the payout at the top of each tier + earnings from previous tiers.)
For every dollar from $0 to $500,000 rate is 0.75%	$3,750 (0.75% x $500,000)	$3,750 at 50% achievement
For every dollar from $500,001 to $1,000,000 rate is 2.25%	$11,250 (2.25% x $500,000)	$15,000 ($3,750 + $11,250) at 100% achievement
For every dollar from $1,000,001 to $1,500,000 rate is 3.00%	$15,000 (3.00% x $500,000)	$30,000 ($3,750 + $11,250 + $15,000) at 150% achievement

Cumulative Payout	Payout for Achievement (Remember: Rate applies to all volume from the first dollar)	
Up to $500,000 the rate is 0.75%	$3,750 at 50% achievement	0.75% x $500,000
Once $1,000,000 is achieved the rate is 2.25% on all volume	$22,500 at 100% achievement	(2.25% x $1,000,000) rate applies to all volume from first dollar (results in payout greater than target for target performance)
And once $1,500,000 is achieved the rate is 3.00% on all volume	$45,000 at 150% achievement	(3% x $1,500,000) rate applies to all volume from first dollar

Using the information from Figure 3-5, Figure 3-6 shows the process used to determine where rates will change, whether the calculation is discrete or cumulative. Figure 3-6a on page 44 illustrates the application of the process to determine the rates if the payout calculation is cumulative. Figure 3-6b on page 45 shows how the process is used to determine rates if the payout calculation is discrete.

Figure 3-6

Determining Ramped Rates

Step	
1. Confirm that payout is available from the first dollar.	In Figure 3-5, payout is made from dollar one
2. Determine if it is financially acceptable to pay at the same rate up to 100% of quota, or if a rate of lesser value is appropriate until a defined level of achievement is reached.	Based on modeling, less than 10% of the salesforce is lower than 50% of quota each year, but at least 50% of quota must be reached for the company to remain viable. Therefore, the payout rate is lower until 50% of quota is reached. To ensure financial viability, 25% of target incentive will be paid at 50% achievement. After 50% of quota is achieved, the rate accelerates in order to pay out 100% of the target incentive opportunity at 100% performance.
3. Determine the number of times the rate should change in total, and in particular above 100% achievement.	Based on competitive practice, the rate should change at least once for over-quota achievement.
4. Confirm the likely "excellence level" to determine the upside tier.	No more than 10% of the salespeople achieve > 150% of quota; 150% is established as the excellence level. Competitive practice and financial modeling indicate that 2 times target incentive should be paid at excellence or 150% of quota.
5. Calculate the base rate (target incentive opportunity divided by quota).	Formula: $\frac{\$15{,}000}{\$1{,}000{,}000}$
6. Confirm if the payout will be discrete or cumulative.	Figure 3-6a shows the formula for determining the rates in a cumulative plan (i.e., with a "lookback" to the first dollar). Figure 3-6b shows the formula for determining the rates in a discrete plan.

Figure 3-6a

Determining Ramped Rates in a Cumulative Plan (with a Lookback)

	Tier 1 Formula	
The company will pay 25% of target incentive for 50% achievement, so the rate up to 50% results in a payout of $3,750, or 1/4 of $15,000. This rate applies to all dollars, from the first dollar of achievement through 50%.	$\frac{\$15{,}000 \times 25\%}{\$1{,}000{,}000 \times 50\%}$	= .75%

	Tier 2 Formula	
The incentive target is paid at 100% achievement. This rate applies to all dollars of achievement, from the first dollar up to 100%.	$\frac{\$15{,}000}{\$1{,}000{,}000}$	= 1.5%

	Tier 3 Formula	
The company will pay 2 times target incentive for 150% achievement, so the total cumulative earnings are $30,000 at 150%. This rate applies to all dollars of achievement from the first dollar.	$\frac{\$15{,}000 \times 2}{\$1{,}000{,}000 \times 1.5}$	= 2.0%

The resulting cumulative commission schedule for this example would look like this:

Cumulative Commission Schedule

Revenue Volume	Cumulative Percent of Target Earned	Cumulative Commission Rate
Up to $500,000	25%	0.75%
Up to $1,000,000	100%	1.50%
Up to $1,500,000	200%	2.00%

Figure 3-6b

Determining Ramped Rates in a Discrete Plan (without a Lookback)

	Tier 1 Formula	
The company will pay 25% of target incentive for 50% achievement, so the rate applies to achievement up to 50%. 50% achievement results in a payout of \$3,750, or 1/4 of \$15,000.	$\frac{\$15,000 \times 25\%}{\$1,000,000 \times 50\%}$	= .75%

	Tier 2 Formula	
The incentive target is paid at 100% achievement. The second rate is applied only to dollars from 50% to 100% achievement. In this example, \$3,750 has been paid at 50%, and the balance of \$11,250 will be earned for the next 50% of achievement.	$\frac{\$15,000 - (\$15,000 \times 25\%)}{\$1,000,000 - (\$1,000,000 \times 50\%)}$	= 2.25%

	Tier 3 Formula	
The company will pay 2 times target incentive for 150% achievement, so the total cumulative earnings are \$30,000 at 150%. Rate 3 is applied only to dollars above 100% achievement.	$\frac{\$15,000}{(\$1,000,000 \times 1.5) - \$1,000,000}$	= 3.0%

The resulting discrete commission schedule for this example would look like this:

Discrete Commission Schedule

Revenue Volume	Discrete Percent of TIC Earned	Discrete Commission Rate
\$0-\$500,000	25%	0.75%
\$500,001-\$1,000,000	75%	2.25%
\$1,000,001-\$1,500,000	100%	3.00%

Figure 3-7 on page 46 provides several examples of ramped rate commission plans based on achievement of a revenue quota:

- Payout from first dollar with progressive ramp
- Payout from first dollar with regressive ramp
- Payout beginning at threshold with progressive ramp
- Payout beginning at threshold with regressive ramp.

Each plan uses a discrete tier payout calculation process. For instance, in the first two examples, \$2,000 is earned for the first tier, and \$5,000 is earned for the second, or \$7,000 total earnings for volume of \$200,000. In the third and fourth

Figure 3-7

Examples of Ramped Commission-Rate Plans

Quota	$200,000
Target Incentive Opportunity	$7,000

Payout from First Dollar (Progressive Ramp)

Discrete Commission Rate	Volume			Discrete Earnings (on each tier)
2.0%	$1	to	$100,000	$2,000
5.0%	$100,001	to	$200,000	$5,000
6.0%	$200,001	to	$300,000	$6,000
7.0%	$300,001	to	$400,000	$7,000

The rate increases for each tier of performance from the first dollar sold. $7,000 is earned at target performance. Earnings accelerate to the most lucrative rate of 7%.

Pay from First Dollar (Regressive Ramp)

Discrete Commission Rate	Volume			Discrete Earnings (on each tier)
2.0%	$1	to	$100,000	$2,000
5.0%	$100,001	to	$200,000	$5,000
4.0%	$200,001	to	$300,000	$4,000
3.0%	$300,001	to	$400,000	$3,000

The rate increases from Tier 1 to Tier 2, where $7,000 or the target incentive opportunity is earned. The rate then plateaus and decreases ("regresses") at higher tiers to manage payout based on corporate objectives.

Payout from Threshold (Progressive Ramp)

Discrete Commission Rate	Volume			Discrete Earnings (on each tier)
0.0%	$1	to	$100,000	$0
7.0%	$100,001	to	$200,000	$7,000
10.0%	$200,001	to	$300,000	$10,000
13.0%	$300,001	to	$400,000	$13,000

Payout begins after $100,000 volume threshold has been achieved. $7,000 is earned at target performance. Earnings accelerate to the most lucrative rate of 13%.

Payout from Threshold (Regressive Ramp)

Discrete Commission Rate	Volume			Discrete Earnings (on each tier)
0.0%	$1	to	$100,000	$0
7.0%	$100,001	to	$200,000	$7,000
6.0%	$200,001	to	$300,000	$6,000
5.0%	$300,001	to	$400,000	$5,000

Payout begins after $100,000 of volume has been sold. $7,000 is earned at target performance. The rate then decreases ("regresses") at higher tiers to manage payout based on corporate objectives.

examples, $7,000 also is earned for volume of $200,000; however, payout begins only on the first dollar *above* the threshold of $100,000.

How to Calculate the Payout

The calculation is based on whether the plan is discrete or cumulative. As described in Figure 3-5, the commission rate applies either to each dollar of volume or each unit in a specified tier, or to all dollars back to dollar one, or all units sold once a new tier is achieved.

Variable or Adjusted Commission

Definition and Typical Use

In an adjusted commission-rate plan, the rates are inconsistent and vary depending on specified variables or performance measures. This approach is used if several types of products or transaction types will be prioritized in the commission structure. More information on adjusted value plans is provided in Chapter 5.

How to Determine the Rate

The rate applied to each transaction is adjusted based on the priority or importance of the product or transaction. In a simple adjusted rate commission plan, the relevant performance measures are weighted based on strategic or financial importance, and that weight (as a portion of 100 percent) is applied to the target incentive opportunity for the job. The result is used to calculate the commission rates for each measure. Figure 3-8 provides an example of establishing the appro-

Figure 3-8

Establishing the Adjusted Commission Rate

Total Corporate Revenue Goal	$130,000,000
Target Incentive Opportunity	$50,000
Number of Salespeople	20

	Revenue Goal	Weight (Importance)	Product IC Opportunity (Target Incentive Opportunity x Weight)	Rate (Product Incentive Opportunity x Number of Salespeople) Divided by Product Revenue Goal
Product A	$10,000,000	20.0%	$10,000	2.000%
Product B	$90,000,000	50.0%	$25,000	0.556%
Product C	$30,000,000	30.0%	$15,000	1.000%
Totals	$130,000,000	100%	**$50,000**	

priate commission rate for three products based on each product's strategic importance and contribution to the total corporate revenue objective.

How to Calculate the Payout

In the simplest adjusted rate commission plan, payout is calculated by product:

Product Volume x Product Rate = Payout

Individual Commission Rate

Definition and Typical Use

An individual commission rate (ICR) plan involves the use of a commission rate that is unique to each person within a specific sales job. An ICR plan may use a fixed-rate approach (where the same rate applies to all sales, but the rate differs by salesperson) or a ramped-rate approach (rates are tiered, with the base rate varying by salesperson).

Essentially, it is a hybrid incentive approach that involves the use of a bonus opportunity with the calculation method of a commission. As such, the ICR has two key characteristics in common with a bonus plan: It has the effect of "evening out" territories in terms of pay, and *it is always used with a quota.* The objective is to ensure that all salespeople in a specific job have the same earnings opportunity, no matter how large or small their territory. ICR plans typically are used:

- As a transition plan (e.g., when a company is moving from a traditional commission plan to a quota-based bonus approach)
- In companies that frequently realign territories
- With larger sales organizations where the industry norm is a commission, but a fixed (or flat) rate commission plan may result in unacceptable behaviors or earnings that are disproportionately high when compared to the value added by the salesperson.

How to Determine the Rate

Two pieces of information are required to set the commission rate for each salesperson:

- The performance goal (i.e., the target or quota)
- The incentive opportunity the company offers for achievement of the performance goal (i.e., the target incentive).

The formula for determining the commission rate is:

$$\frac{\text{Individual Target Incentive Opportunity}}{\text{Individual Performance Goal}}$$

Figure 3-9
Individual Commission-Rate Examples

	Salesperson A	Salesperson B
Quota	$1,000,000	$2,000,000
Target Incentive Opportunity	$50,000	$50,000
ICR	5.0%	2.5%

Figure 3-10
Ramped Rate Commission Plan with ICRs

	Salesperson A
Quota	$1,000,000
Target Incentive Opportunity	$50,000
ICR	5.0%

Progressive Ramp (Cumulative)				
Commission Rate	Earnings	Volume		
2.5%	$12,500	$1	to	$500,000
5.0%	$50,000	$500,001	to	$1,000,000
7.5%	$112,500	$1,000,001	to	$1,500,000

	Salesperson B
Quota	$2,000,000
Target Incentive Opportunity	$50,000
ICR	2.5%

Progressive Ramp (Cumulative)				
Commission Rate	Earnings	Volume		
1.25%	$12,500	$1	to	$1,000,000
2.50%	$50,000	$1,000,001	to	$2,000,000
3.75%	$112,500	$2,000,001	to	$3,000,000

Figure 3-9 on page 49 provides to examples of the application of this formula using a fixed rate approach. Figure 3-10 on page 49 illustrates a ramped rate plan that uses ICRs.

How to Calculate the Payout

Payout for each salesperson is calculated with his/her own rate or rate table based on the type of plan (fixed or ramped) as described in the previous relevant sections.

Combination Ramped Rate and Adjusted Rate Commission Plans

An alternative to using either a ramped rate or an adjusted rate is to develop a design that uses both approaches together to determine the operative commission rate. One example is the use of adjusted rates that ramp based on goal achievement. The rates for this kind of plan are calculated based on the concepts previously described that relate to how a ramped rate is calculated, and the factors that affect adjusted commission rates. Using the example in Figure 3-8, Figure 3-11 illustrates how the adjusted rates could be ramped if both goal achievement and product priority are used to determine the rate(s).

Establishing the Payout Line

As illustrated in Figure 3-4, a payout line (or payout curve) is a graphic representation of pay earned at various levels of achievement from the first dollar earned. For a fixed-rate commission plan, the payout line is linear with a constant shape. (See Figure 3-12.)

However, for other types of commission plans, determining the payout line is a critical step in establishing the incentive available at each level of achievement. At least two, and optimally three, of the following points of comparison are used to illustrate the payout line:

Figure 3-11

Adjusted Commission Rate that Is Ramped

Percent of Quota		Progressive Ramp (Cumulative)			
		Product A	Product B	Product C	
	0%-50%	1.000%	0.278%	0.500%	
	>50%-100%	2.000%	0.556%	1.000%	(rates from Fig 3-8)
	>100%-150%	3.000%	0.833%	1.500%	
	>150%	4.000%	1.111%	2.000%	

- The point at which payout begins (the threshold)
- The target performance level
- The point at which the designed upside is paid
- Each interim point at which the rate of payout changes.

As described in Chapter 2, the performance range (threshold, target, excellence) must be defined as a critical first step in establishing the payout line. The payout at each level is modeled, as described in Figure 3-6. Frequently, either a progressive or regressive payout line is desired—and must be designed for. Once confirmed, various techniques can be used to ensure that the payout line as designed is consistent with the financial objectives agreed upon.

With a progressive payout line, the rate increases as performance exceeds defined levels (as illustrated in Figure 3-4). To increase payout, either of two mathematical operations can be used: multiplication or addition. A regressive payout line means that the rate decelerates at some defined level of performance. To achieve this, limitations must be built into the plan.

In either case, the simplest adjustment to make is in the commission rate available at each performance level. As described, the rates can be calculated based on the desired financial outcome at each point. Additional techniques include:

- A multiplier, which adjusts the payout for one performance measure up or down based on achievement of another performance measure (described further in Chapter 5)
- A hurdle or gate, which requires some predetermined level of performance

Figure 3-12
Illustration of Linear Payout Line (Fixed-Rate Commission Plan)

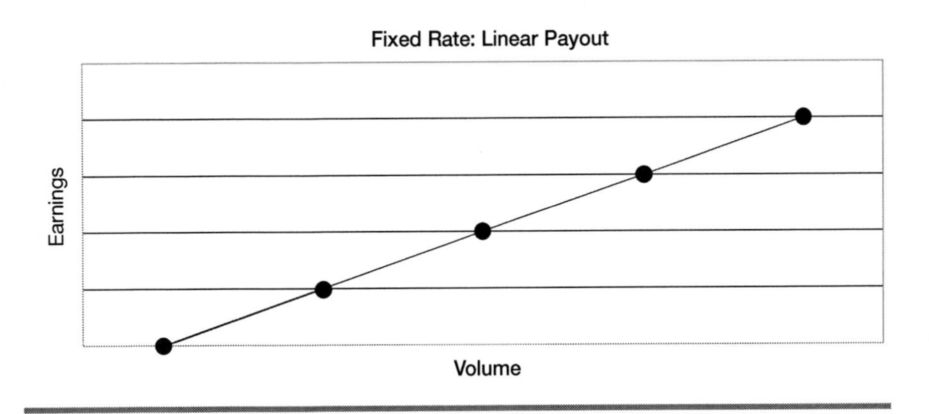

against one measure before a specified level of payout is available for another (also described in Chapter 5)
- Sales crediting acceleration or deceleration, in which each dollar of volume is worth more or less than a dollar based on defined factors, such as product importance, product availability or associated margin (as described in Chapter 2).

How to Finalize the Commission-Plan Formula

While a commission plan directly relates incentive pay to volume, several factors should be considered to finalize the commission formula:
- Is the incentive opportunity appropriate and competitive? This should be confirmed at the start of the design process because the value of the incentive opportunity is a key factor in determining the rate or rates.
- What is the company's key objective this year? The second factor in rate determination is the denominator of the equation and ties directly to corporate success.
- As a percent of sales, how much can we afford to spend to achieve our objective? While the formula is straightforward, companies sometimes find that some adjustment to rates is required. There may be two reasons:
  - Achievement of the company's profit target will not be possible with the same calculated rate for all products or all types of sales, or
  - There is more margin or profit available to be shared with the salesforce if the company's revenue and margin objectives are achieved.
- What behaviors will the commission motivate, and are these consistent with our company's objectives and philosophy? This factor cannot be addressed through financial analysis. However, because each type of commission plan implies a different management message about priorities and required behavior, companies with little experience in compensating salespeople may want to test the approach in a small geography. This ensures that the behavior motivated by the plan is delivering the financial objectives required while delivering the customer results necessary for ongoing success.

Summing Up

Commission formulas have an important place in the portfolio of techniques used to design effective sales incentive plans. These kinds of plans generally are easy to understand and focus the salesperson's efforts on the measures against which commissions are calculated. However, commissions also may encourage self-serving or autonomous behaviors, and make changes to customer coverage based on new business objectives or a revised sales strategy difficult. Therefore, selection of this approach should be based on a clear, well-defined strategic direction from management about the corporate objectives to be supported by the plan, and the culture and behavior that are consistent with the company's philosophy.

Once the strategic direction and sales job charter have been confirmed, developing the formula requires active involvement of a knowledgeable design team including HR, sales management and finance to complete the design, related financial analysis and support documentation.

Several alternatives are available to the team that has the job of developing the commission plan, ranging from a simple fixed rate to more complex approaches, such as an adjusted rate that ramps. The selection of the most appropriate approach should be based on the behavior and results required, the sales deployment model, the availability of systems that can track results and administer the plan, and financial viability.

Chapter 4
Bonuses

Bonus is pay calculated as a percentage of salary, salary range midpoint or a target dollar award value. The incentive is calculated and paid based on the relationship of actual performance (sum of many transactions) to a goal. Bonus plans always have a "planned dollar" payout against an established objective. These programs support a relative measurement system—payout depends on performance compared to individual or group goals.

When to Use Bonuses

As indicated in Chapter 3, management objectives and the selling environment are key considerations in the selection of the appropriate type of formula for a sales incentive compensation plan. Bonuses typically are used:

- In a moderate to low-growth or maturing industry
- Where there is a focus on multiple business objectives, including retaining sales/accounts
- With a sales process that is consultative, and the seller works with other resources throughout the process
- Where there is unequal sales potential, and sales resources are assigned geographically or with unequal account portfolios
- In a rapidly changing sales environment in which territories/account assignments change periodically, sales deployment is changing and additional resources are being added to the organization
- When qualitative goals are important to sales success and realistic quotas or goals are relatively easier to set because of sales history and experience.

Bonuses frequently are used as the appropriate approach to compensating salespeople in business-to-business sales, such as enterprise software, professional services, chemicals and situations in which the "sale" cannot be attributed directly to the "seller," such as pharmaceutical and semiconductor sales.

Types of Bonuses

Bonus and commission formulas are similar in that they both range from simple to complex in their calculation, as illustrated in Figure 4-1.

Flat or Fixed Bonus

Definition and Typical Use

In a flat or fixed bonus plan, the bonus rate does not vary. This is the simplest bonus to develop and explain because the incentive opportunity available for achieving the specified objective is one specified dollar amount. It also is simple because the performance range contains only one point (i.e., target). In this way, the bonus is binary—either you achieve the goal and earn the flat bonus, or you don't.

This type of bonus most often is used in contests or special performance incentives for the field (SPIFFs), and rarely is used as the single incentive-compensation component, except as a transition technique to facilitate the use of effective variable pay. A single rate bonus may, however, be used as one component of an incentive compensation plan if a qualitative measure, such as strategic objectives (also known as key sales objectives or KSOs, management by objectives or MBOs), is included in the plan, and payout is intended only for "target" performance. Figure 4-2 provides examples of situations in which a flat bonus might be used.

How to Determine the Rate

Because the same rate applies for all salespeople eligible for the bonus plan, the information required to set the rate is as follows:

- The key metric that will be rewarded is identified or selected (e.g., new accounts, achievement of new product volume).

Figure 4-1
Complexity Spectrum

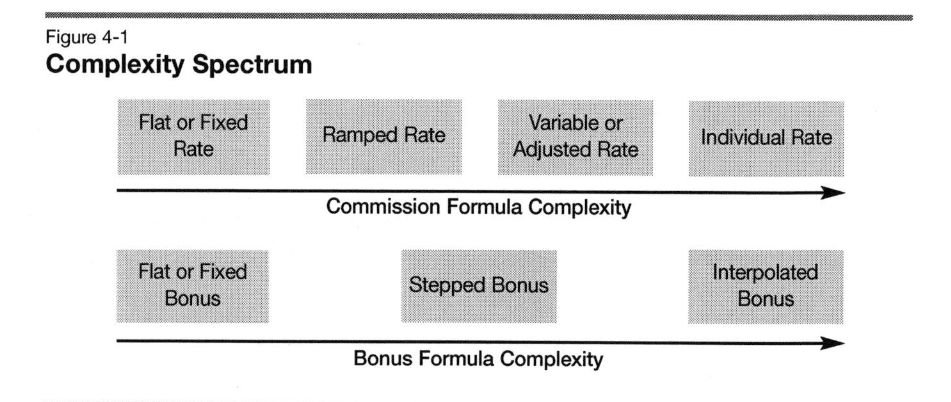

Figure 4-2
Examples of Fixed Rate Bonuses

'Add On' Opportunity	At-Risk Pay
Cash award(s) paid at 100% achievement of objectives in addition to the total cash compensation for the job	The variable portion of a salesperson's total cash compensation that is paid at 100% achievement of (implicit or explicit) objectives
Short-term sales contest or SPIFF	Always related to achievement of a specified goal or quota
Examples: • $1,000 for the territory's first new account • $5,000 for achievement of product sales goal	**Examples:** • Guaranteed single rate bonus for the first period a new salesforce is deployed; for example, 25% of the annual incentive opportunity budgeted for this salesforce • Single-rate bonus available to a job newly eligible for sales compensation for achievement of objectives; for example, $5,000 if quarterly sales objective is achieved • Provided as the opportunity for achievement of KSOs or MBOs; for example, $5,000 if documented and approved KSOs have been achieved and documentation has been submitted

- The incentive opportunity the company offers for achievement relative to that metric is defined.
- The expected participation rate is estimated (if applicable).

The basic formula for determining the bonus rate is:

$$\frac{\text{Total Budget for Bonus Plan}}{\text{Total Number of Payouts}}$$

Figure 4-3 on page 58 provides three examples of how this formula can be applied.

How to Calculate the Payout

The calculation for determining incentive payout is simplest with a fixed or flat rate bonus because a fixed dollar amount is paid each time the specified milestone is achieved by a salesperson. This, too, is illustrated in Figure 4-3 examples.

Stepped (Tiered) Bonus

Definition and Typical Use

With a stepped or tiered bonus, the payout changes after each milestone or distinct

Figure 4-3

Examples of Calculating Fixed Bonus Payout Opportunity

New 'Product A' Contest	
Total budget for Product A contest	$200,000
Total number of salespeople	32
Expected participation	90%
Bonus opportunity = $\frac{\text{Total Budget}}{\text{(Number of Salespeople x Expected Participation)}}$	$6,944
Payout for achieving product goal ($6,944 rounded)	$7,000

New-Accounts Contest	
Total new revenue required	$1,000,000
Average revenue per new account	$50,000
Number of new accounts required	20
New-account margin (first year)	4%
Budget for new-accounts contest (company will spend margin to gain new-account revenue stream) Budget = 4% x $1,000,000	$40,000
Payout for first new account in a territory $\left(\frac{\text{Budget for contest}}{\text{Number of New Accounts Required}}\right)$	$2,000

KSO Bonus*	
Total target sales incentive opportunity	$20,000
Weight of KSO component	25%
Annual payout for achievement	$5,000

*In this example, there is no payout for above or below target.

level within the performance range is achieved. As with commissions, a specific payout rate typically is determined for "target" achievement, and different payouts are provided for sales below or above target. "Target" may be a specified sales volume, a milestone or a percent of quota achievement.

A tiered bonus is designed to pay out based on a discrete event or on a range of achievement. It may be used with qualitative incentive plan components (e.g., strategic objectives)—if the company has concluded that achievement can be differentiated further than a binary outcome of "achieved versus not achieved"—and in cases in which it is difficult to validate whether that performance can be tracked and credited within 1 percent or 2 percent. Figure 4-4 provides two examples of this type of bonus.

As illustrated in the first example, quota achievement at any point between 75 percent and 95 percent of quota results in a payout of $5,000. However, achievement within five percentage points of target (up or down) results in a payout of $10,000. The second example is a simple way to approach payout on KSO achieve-

Figure 4-4
Stepped or Tiered Bonus

Quota Achievement Bonus Example		
< 75% of quota achieved	No payout	
75%-95% of quota achieved	$5,000	(no matter where achievement falls in the range)
95.1%-105% of quota achieved	$10,000	(no matter where achievement falls in the range)
> 105% of quota achieved	$12,500	(no matter where achievement falls in the range)

KSO Achievement Bonus Example

Each KSO has specific performance milestones associated with threshold, target and excellent performance. Each KSO has a defined incentive opportunity.

Achievement Level	Payout as a Percent of KSO's Opportunity
Threshold	50%
Target	100%
Excellent	125%

ment: Each KSO is assigned an incentive opportunity, and payout is based on the level of achievement for each KSO individually. See Chapter 5 for more in-depth treatment of a KSO bonus.

How to Determine the Rate

Rate determination is based on the value of the component as a percent of the total target incentive opportunity. Figure 4-5 on page 60 provides an example of the calculation using a two-component incentive plan. Each component is rewarded based on a stepped bonus. The data required to set the rates are:

- The incentive opportunity the company offers for target achievement
- The relative proportion of the incentive opportunity allocated to each component (i.e., performance-measure weighting)
- Financial modeling to determine the minimum performance level that must be achieved before a bonus can be paid (threshold) for the relevant component (this analysis typically is completed by finance)
- Financial modeling to determine sales performance that is in the 90th percentile (top 10 percent) of all individuals whose performance is being measured (excellence) for each component (this analysis is completed by the function responsible for plan administration and reporting)
- Confirmation of the leverage or upside associated with performance at this level for each component.

In the example, the relative bonus at each level for each component must be deter-

Figure 4-5
Establishing the Bonus Rates

Step 1: Determine the incentive opportunity.	Total Target Cash Compensation	$50,000
	Salary/Incentive Mix	60/40
	Incentive Opportunity	$20,000
Step 2: Determine the value of each component.	Achievement of Quota Weight	75% $15,000
	Achievement of KSOs Weight	25% $5,000
Step 3: Determine the threshold for each component.	Threshold for Quota Achievement	quota must be achieved for any payout
	Threshold for KSO	based on each KSO
Step 3: Determine the upside value and definition of excellence.	Leverage	2
	Total Incentive at Excellence	$40,000 or an additional $20,000
	Excellence for Quota Achievement	150%
	Excellence for KSO	based on each KSO
Step 4: Calculate the relative upside for each component.	Quota Achievement Upside	225% $33,750
	KSO Update	125% $6,250

Quota Achievement-2 rates: Payout available for quota achievement (target) and excellence or greater	**Quota Achievement Bonus**	
	0%-99.9%	0
	100%-150%	$15,000
	>150%	$33,750
KSO Achievement Example 1: Two rates for each KSO	**KSO Bonus: Example 1 - Discrete KSOs**	
	KSO 1 = 50% of KSO target	
	Target	$2,500
	Excellence	$3,125
	KSO 2 = 50% of KSO target	
	Target	$2,500
	Excellence	$3,125
KSO Achievement Example 2: Achievement is aggregated with payout for achievement of 1 KSO, 2 KSOs and 2 achieved + excellence in at least 1	**KSO Bonus: Example 2 - Point Table**	
	Total Points (to provide basis for calculation)	100
	KSO 1 = 50% of KSO target	50
	KSO 2 = 50% of KSO target	50
	Excellence milestones defined for each-additional 25 points each	50
	50-99 points achieved	$2,500
	100-125 points achieved	$5,000
	> 125 points achieved	$6,250

mined based on the incentive opportunity for that component and the total leverage or upside that will be paid at excellence. Total leverage (upside) is two times target, quota achievement is weighted at three times KSO achievement (75 percent and 25 percent) and the upside that is available for KSO achievement is 125 percent. The upside leverage percentage for the quota-achievement component is calculated in Step 4 of Figure 4-5 based on these factors, and the formula is:

$$\frac{(\text{Total Upside at Excellence} - \text{Upside for KSOs})}{\text{Target Incentive for Quota Achievement}}$$

Using this formula, the math to arrive at the upside leverage percentage for the quota-achievement component works out as follows:

$$\frac{(\$40{,}000 - \$6{,}250)}{\$15{,}000} = 225\%$$

In the example, no payout is available for quota achievement of less than 100 percent. At performance of 100 percent to 150 percent, the target incentive is paid. For achievement above 150 percent of quota, 225 percent of the target incentive for that component is paid.

Determination of the rates available for KSO achievement is based on the way in which achievement is expressed for that component. As illustrated, approaches may include:

- Treatment of each KSO as a separate plan component
- Aggregation of achievement based on some type of scoring system (in this case, weighted KSOs with points assigned and payout based on points achieved).

How to Calculate the Payout

Payout is determined based on the milestone or achievement range that has been reached. For example, using the plan illustrated in Figure 4-5:

- If the percent of quota achieved lies at any point from 100 percent to 150 percent, the payout is $15,000.
- If the KSO uses the approach illustrated in Figure 4-5 as Example 1, and achievement is target for KSO 1 and excellence for KSO 2, the payout is $2,500 for KSO 1 and $3,125 for KSO 2.
- The total payout for this person is $15,000 + $2,500 + $3,125 = $20,625.

  Again, using the plan illustrated in Figure 4-5:
- If the percent of quota achieved is greater than 150 percent, then payout for that component is $33,750 (calculated as $15,000 x 2.25).
- If the approach for KSOs used is Example 2 and the achievement is excellence

for KSO 1 (75 points) and target for KSO 2 (50 points), the payout is $5,000 (excellence was not achieved for both; the total points achieved equal 125).

- Total payout: $33,750 + $5,000 = $38,750.

Interpolated Bonus

Definition and Typical Use

This type of bonus provides a defined value (dollars, percent of base or percent of target) for each percentage point of quota or goal achieved. If a bonus is included in the sales incentive plan, it typically is this type and frequently is known as a "rate per point" plan. The plan may use a cumulative or discrete payout formula.

As described in Part 3, if the plan is cumulative (also known as a plan with a "lookback" or "clawback"), incentive paid versus incentive earned is recalculated at defined intervals (i.e., the rate applies to all points from threshold to the point of achievement over subsequent periods). If the plan is discrete, then the rate per point achieved is applicable only for the related range of achievement. An interpolated bonus "evens out" payout across territories with different potential, and should only be used if the organization has the ability to set accurate and credible quotas.

How to Determine the Rate

The rate available for each percentage point of achievement is determined with a formula that uses the incentive earned for the range as the numerator and the number of points in the range of achievement as the denominator, as follows:

$$\frac{\text{Total Dollars Available for Range}}{\text{Number of Points in Range}}$$

To determine the numerator and denominator, the following factors must be considered:

- The incentive opportunity the company offers for achieving target
- Financial modeling to determine at what point of achievement bonus can be paid (e.g., from first dollar or at some point of quota achievement that is defined as the minimum level of performance that must be achieved before an incentive can be paid [threshold])
- Financial modeling to determine sales performance that reflects the 90th percentile (top 10 percent) of all individuals whose performance is being measured (excellence)
- Confirmation of the leverage or upside associated with performance at this level
- Determination of whether discrete or cumulative performance measurement is most appropriate for the sales environment.

Figure 4-6 shows a simple plan that uses an interpolated bonus ("rate per point") formula. This plan is discrete; that is, the rate for each range *applies only to achievement within that range.*

In this example, the mix has been defined as 80-percent salary and 20-percent incentive; the result is a target incentive opportunity expressed in dollars of $20,000. The upside available at 125-percent quota achievement is 2.5 times target, or $50,000 in total ($20,000 for target performance, $30,000 for excellence performance).

The formula for calculating the rate for each range is as follows:

- There is a range of achievement below which no incentive is earned (below 80 percent); the threshold is 80 percent. Therefore, there are 20 points of achievement from threshold to 100 percent. The formula for calculating the incentive per point for this first range is:

$$\frac{\text{(Incentive at Target)}}{(100\% - \text{Threshold }\%) \times 100}$$

OR

$$\frac{\$20{,}000}{(100\% - 80\%) \times 100} = \text{\$1,000 Per Point from Threshold to Target}$$

Figure 4-6

Interpolated Bonus—Discrete Ranges

Annual Compensation		
	Mix	
Annual Base Salary	80%	$80,000
Target Incentive	20%	$20,000
Leverage	2.5	
Total Target Cash Compensation		**$100,000**

Performance Measures & Weights		
Measure	**Weight**	**Target**
Total Sales vs. Quota	100%	$20,000
Total Weight	**100%**	

Bonus Table			
Total Sales vs. Quota			
% of Quota Achieved	**Annual Payout per %**	**Annual Payout for Level**	
0%-80%	$0	$0	
80%-100%	$1,000	$20,000	20 points x $1,000
100%-125%	$1,200	+ $30,000	25 points x $1,200
and beyond		= $50,000	at 125%

- For the next range of achievement, the same approach is used, but the upside must be taken into account in the formula:

$$\frac{\text{Incentive at Target x Leverage Multiple}}{\text{(Excellence Percent Minus 100\%) x 100}}$$

OR

$$\frac{(\$20{,}000 \times 2.5) - \$20{,}000}{(125\% - 100\%) \times 100} = \text{\$1,200 Per Point from Target to Excellence}$$

The incentive opportunity also may be expressed as a percent of salary, as shown in Figure 4-7. In this example, the value of each point is expressed as a percent of salary, as well. Here is the formula to calculate the rates per point in this example:

- First, calculate incentive to be earned for target performance as a percent of the base salary ($20,000 target incentive / $80,000 base salary = 25%)
- For the first range, the formula is:

$$\frac{25\%}{(100\% - 80\%) \times 100} = \text{1.25\% of Salary Per Point Achieved from Threshold to Target}$$

Figure 4-7

Incentive Opportunity as Percent of Salary

Annual Compensation			
	Mix		
Annual Base Salary	80%	$80,000	
Target Incentive	20%	$20,000	or 25% of salary
Leverage	2.5		or 62.5% of salary
Total Target Cash Compensation		**$100,000**	

Performance Measures & Weights		
Measure	**Weight**	**Target %**
Total Sales vs. Quota	100%	25%
Total Weight	**100%**	

Bonus Table			
Total Sales vs. Quota			
% of Quota Achieved	**Annual Payout per %**	**Annual Payout for Level**	
0%-80%	0.00%	$0	
80%-100%	1.25% of salary	$20,000	20 pts x 1.25% x $80,000
100%-125%	1.50% of salary	+ $30,000	25 pts x 1.50% x $80,000
and beyond		= $50,000	at 125%

- For the second range, the formula is:

$$\frac{(25\% \times 2.5) - 25\%}{(125\% - 100\%) \times 100} = \text{1.5\% of Salary for Each Point Achieved from Target to Excellence}$$

How to Calculate the Payout

The formula for determining payout is based on whether the plan has discrete ranges or the payout is cumulative. Figure 4-8 illustrates a payout that is discrete (i.e., each rate applies only to the points within that range).

Figure 4-9 on page 66 illustrates payout that is cumulative (i.e., the rate for each range applies to all points of achievement from threshold forward).

How to Finalize the Plan Formula

Chapter 3 provides a complete description of the factors to consider and the techniques that can be used to establish the payout line. Once the optimal payout line is

Figure 4-8

Interpolated Bonus with Discrete Ranges—Payout Illustration

Target Incentive $20,000
Leverage 2.5

% of Quota Achieved	Annual Payout per %	Annual Payout for Level
0%-80%	$0	$0
80%-100%	$1,000	$20,000
100%-125% and beyond	$1,200	$30,000

Discrete Payout Ranges For every % achieved	Rate is	Payout for Range	Total Payout	
0.00%-80.00%	$0	$0	$0	
80.01%-100%	$1,000	$20,000	$20,000	
100.01%-125% and beyond	$1,200	$30,000	$50,000 at 125%	$20,000+$30,000

Payout Illustrations

Achievement	Payout	Formula	
85%	$5,000	((85%-80%) x 100) x $1,000	or 5 pts x $1,000
98%	$18,000	((98%-80%) x 100) x $1,000	or 18 pts x $1,000
102%	$22,400	$20,000+((102%-100%) x 100) x $1,200	or target of $20,000 +(2 pts x $1,200)
127%	$52,400	$50,000+((127%-125%) x 100) x $1,200	or excellence of $50,000 +(2 pts x $1,200)

Figure 4-9

Interpolated Bonus with Cumulative Ranges—Payout Illustration

Target Incentive	$20,000
Leverage	2.5

% of Quota Achieved	Annual Payout per %	Cumulative Payout Amount
0%-80%	$0	$0
80%-100%	$1,000	$20,000
100%-125% and beyond	$1,111	$50,000

Cumulative Payout Ranges For every % achieved	Rate is	Total Payout
0.00%-80.00%	$0	$0
80.01%-100%	$1,000	$20,000
100.01%-125% and beyond	$1,111.11	$50,000 at 125%

Payout Illustrations

Achievement	Payout	Formula	
85%	$5,000	((85%-80%) x 100) x $1,000	or 5 pts x $1,000
98%	$18,000	((98%-80%) x 100) x $1,000	or 18 pts x $1,000
102%	$24,444	((102%-80%) x 100) x $1,111.11	or 22 pts x $1,111.11
127%	$52,222	((127%-80%) x 100) x $1,111.11	or 47 pts x $1,111.11

established, the plan formula needs to be finalized. Because a bonus plan directly relates incentive pay to achievement of one or several defined goals (also known as quota, objective, plan or budget), several factors should be considered to finalize the formula:

- **Is the incentive opportunity appropriate and competitive?** This should be confirmed at the start of the design process because the value of the incentive opportunity is a key factor in determining the rate or rates.
- **As a percent of sales, how much can the company afford to spend to achieve its objectives?** While the formula is straightforward, companies sometimes find that some adjustment is needed to the rate or rates above and below target based on financial viability, leadership requirements and the behaviors necessary to achieve plan.
- **Is the plan rewarding appropriately for performance**? To answer this question optimally, modeling should be completed based on historic performance and projected scenarios.

Summing Up

Bonus plans are used in sales situations in which it is desirable to relate the incentive payout to the relationship of actual performance to a goal and to equalize the earnings potential across territories. The ability to set a goal and, thus, reward for its achievement is a central consideration in the decision to use a bonus plan for salespeople. A bonus formula also is used to ensure alignment across positions, and is the approach that must be used if the achievement of nonfinancial or qualitative objectives is critical to business success.

There are a variety of formulas from which to choose when relating goal performance to the incentive payout opportunity. Flat or fixed bonuses, stepped or tiered rate bonuses and interpolated bonuses are the three most common plan types. Because these bonus formulas range from simple to complex, it is important to ensure that the plan calculation follows prescribed protocol.

Chapter 5
Advanced Incentive Techniques

This chapter delves into the more advanced incentive techniques often required for complex selling models. These techniques can be appropriate and helpful when various sales priorities compete with one another (e.g., volume and profit). As such, this part of the book focuses more on illustrations of incentive techniques rather than the math that is consistently used in formula development. For many of the illustrations shown in this chapter, the formula calculations have been discussed elsewhere.

Using Commission and Bonus in the Same Plan

It is common to employ a bonus and commission in the same plan. This is particularly true when different sales priorities and their associated performance measures reflect different stages in market maturation or the organization's life cycle.

For example, consider an organization with a strong base of imbedded business that is entering a new market with little existing business. If a single "blended" sales role will have existing-account management and new-account acquisition responsibilities, a quota-based bonus may be appropriate to reward the existing-account aspect of the role, while a commission may be used to reward new-account sales results. Figure 5-1 illustrates a sales compensation plan that would be appropriate for this type of job.

The two components of this plan are:

- A quota-based bonus with payout illustrated as a percent of the target bonus for each tier of achievement. Payout can be interpolated for each percent in the relevant tier.
- A tiered commission with a higher rate available for performance above target.

For this plan, the quota-based bonus with a high minimum-performance threshold makes sense for the existing-account measure, as the large base of imbedded business will undoubtedly aid in setting reasonable quotas. However, for the new market this company is entering, there is no historical basis for sound quota setting. Therefore, a commission approach—paid from first dollar on the basis of new-account revenue volume without an explicit quota—makes sense.

In the combination commission-bonus plan illustrated in Figure 5-1, the two performance measures are "unlinked." That is, the existing-account quota attainment bonus and the new-account revenue commission do not impact each other mathematically. Because the measures are unlinked, strong performance on one measure at the expense of the other measure (e.g., outstanding existing-account quota attainment and marginal new-account volume) is not inherently penalized. For example, with strong existing-account quota attainment performance, the sales representative can more than offset the lack of commission earnings from subpar new-account performance. When management seeks to reinforce a more balanced perspective across two or more competing measures, then a "linked" technique is required.

Linked-Formula Calculations

In a complex sales environment, management may ask the salesforce to achieve multiple, yet potentially competing, objectives. For example:

- As prices erode in a competitive marketplace, the company may require not only volume, but volume at an established margin.
- When a new product is introduced, focus is necessary on the traditional or in-line products (which may be considered commoditized) and the new product (which may compete for shelf space or share of customer spend).
- While repeat business is important to keep a strong base, growth requires attention to gaining new accounts or customers.

In these situations, a simple "unlinked" plan formula may not be effective in communicating the desired message to the sales organization. An alternative approach is to use a "linked" formula, meaning that payout for the achievement

Figure 5-1
Combination Bonus-Commission Plan

Annual Compensation	Mix	
Annual Base Salary	70%	$63,000
Target Incentive	30%	$27,000
Target Cash Compensation	**100%**	**$90,000**
Leverage Multiple	2.50	$67,500

Quota	
Existing-account revenue	$2,200,000
New-account revenue	$240,000

Performance Measures & Weights

Measure	Weight	Target	Incentive Formula	Cap
Existing-account revenue versus quota	60%	$16,200	Step bonus	None
New-account revenue	40%	$10,800	Variable rate commission	None
Total Value at Target	**100%**	**$27,000**		

1. Existing-Account Bonus

Performance Range	YTD % of Quota Achieved	Bonus Rate (% of Target Bonus)
Threshold	85.0%-89.9%	40%
	90.0%-94.9%	60%
	95.0%-99.9%	80%
Target	100.0%-104.9%	100%
	105.0%-109.9%	150%
	110.0%-114.9%	200%
Excellence	115.0%	250%
Above Excellence	115.1% +	5%*

*Bonus rate above excellence is the percent of target bonus earned for each percentage point of quota achieved.

2. New-Account Commission

Performance Range	Monthly New-Account Revenue Volume	Commission Rate (% of Revenue)
Up to Target	$0-$20,000	4.5%
Above Target	$20,001 +	6.8%

of one performance objective is tied to achievement of another objective. This can be accomplished by using one or more of three techniques.

Hurdles

A hurdle, or "gate," requires some defined level of achievement in one performance measure before payout is made for another measure. The performance measure used as a hurdle or gate may have an incentive value or weight, or the measure can be used only as a hurdle or requirement for payout on another measure, and thus it has no incentive weight or value. However, in each case it is considered an integral component of the incentive plan.

Figures 5-2a and 5-2b on pages 73 and 74 provide two examples of formulas that include a hurdle. In each example, the target incentive is $50,000, the performance measures are total sales versus quota and variable margin growth, and payout for total sales versus quota is a dollar per point of achievement bonus, calculated based on the target incentive for each tier.

For the two examples, the hurdle mechanism varies based on the message management wants to enforce through the sales compensation plan. In Example A in Figure 5-2a, Vvariable-Margin Growth is the hurdle and has no incentive value. That is, the weight is zero. However, to be eligible to receive overachievement pay on the sales-versus-quota bonus, a plan participant must have achieved the specified variable-margin growth hurdle of 2 percent over prior year.

Advantages of the hurdle formula as illustrated here are:

- The ability to incorporate another performance measure (the hurdle) without diminishing the incentive weight allocated to any of the other measures in the plan, and
- The ability to appropriately limit pay based on the growth of variable margin without "capping" the plan (i.e., overachievement is available assuming the hurdle is achieved).

In Example B in Figure 5-2b, both variable-margin growth and total sales are critical elements of the incentive plan, with equal weights (50 percent of the target incentive). However, to receive any payout on the Variable Margin component, a plan participant must have achieved 100 percent of his/her total sales quota.

Multipliers

A multiplier adjusts payout on one performance measure based on some level of achievement of another measure. Positive adjustment generally is preferred, although adjustment up or down can be used to ensure financial viability of the plan. As in the case of the hurdle, the performance measure used as a multiplier can

Figure 5-2a

Hurdle Examples

Annual Compensation

	Mix	
Annual Base Salary	50%	$50,000
Target Incentive	50%	$50,000
Target Cash Compensation	**100%**	**$100,000**
Leverage Multiple	2.50	$125,000

Quota

Total Sales	$5,000,000
Variable Margin Growth	2.0%

Example A

Message: Variable Margin must increase to fuel company growth.

Hurdle: Variable Margin in aggregate must increase in the assignment by 2% for the plan participant to be eligible for any overachievement payout based on Total Sales vs. Quota.

Performance Measures & Weights

Measure	Weight	Target $	Incentive Formula	
Total Sales vs. Quota	100%	$50,000	Rate-per-point bonus	
Variable-Margin Growth	0%	$0	Hurdle	At least 2% growth required for any overachievement to be paid
Total Value at Target	**100%**	**$50,000**		

1. Total Sales vs. Quota Bonus

% of Quota Achieved	Annual Payout per % Achievement	Annual Payout for Level	Total Incentive Payout
0%-50%	$0	$0	$0
50%-100%	$1,000	$50,000	$50,000
100%-125% and beyond	$3,000	$75,000	$125,000

Payout Illustrations

- 125% of Total Sales vs. Quota is achieved
- Variable Margin has grown 0.5%
- Payout is $50,000 (no overachievement is available because Variable Margin has not grown by 2% or more)

- 125% of Total Sales vs. Quota is achieved
- Variable Margin has grown 2.5%
- Payout is $125,000 (overachievement is available because Variable Margin has grown by 2% or more)

Figure 5-2b

Hurdle Examples

Example B

Message: Volume is necessary to ensure plant fill, which is required for ongoing profitability.

Hurdle: No payout is available for Variable Margin unless 100% of the Total Sales Quota is achieved by the plan participant.

Performance Measures & Weights

Measure	Weight	Target	Incentive Formula	
Total Sales vs. Quota	50%	$25,000	Rate-per-point bonus and hurdle	100% required for VM bonus payout
Variable Margin Growth	50%	$25,000	Step bonus	
Total Value at Target	**100%**	**$50,000**		

1. Total Sales vs. Quota Bonus

% of Quota Achieved	Annual Payout per % Achievement	Annual Payout for Level	Total Annual Payout
0.0%-50.0%	$0	$0	$0
50.1%-100.0%	$500	$25,000	$25,000
100.1%-125.0% and beyond	$1,500	$37,500	$62,500

2. Variable-Margin Growth Bonus

Achievement	Annual Payout for Level	Total Annual Payout
0% or less	$0	$0
0.1%-1.0%	$5,000	$5,000
1.1%-2.0%	$20,000	$25,000
>2%	$37,500	$62,500

Payout Illustrations

- <50% of Total Sales vs. Quota is achieved
- Variable Margin has grown 2%
- Payout is 0. The Total Sales Quota hurdle of 100% has not been achieved, so no Variable Margin bonus is available, and there is no payout for Total Sales unless the threshold is achieved.

- 100% of Total Sales vs. Quota is achieved
- Variable Margin has grown 1.5%
- Payout is $50,000, $25,000 for Total Sales and $25,000 for Variable-Margin growth (payout is available on both measures because Total Sales Quota has been achieved)

either have an incentive value or weight, or it can have a weight of zero. The latter is the case if the multiplier value at target achievement of that measure is one; that is, the earned incentive on the other plan component or components is multiplied by one, and is neither increased nor decreased. Figure 5-3 illustrates this concept.

For under-target variable-margin performance, the incentive payout for total sales is adjusted down, and for over-target performance the incentive payout on total sales is adjusted up. At target-variable margin performance, the incentive for total sales is not adjusted.

Figure 5-3

Multiplier Example

Annual Compensation		
	Mix	
Annual Base Salary	50%	$50,000
Target Incentive	50%	$50,000
Target Cash Compensation	**100%**	**$100,000**
Leverage Multiple	2.50	$125,000

Quota	
Total Sales:	$5,000,000
Variable-Margin Growth:	2.0%

Performance Measures & Weights			
Measure	**Weight**	**Target**	**Incentive Formula**
Total Sales vs. Quota	100%	$50,000	Rate-per-point bonus
Variable-Margin Growth	0%	$0	Multiplier
Total Value at Target	**100%**	**$50,000**	

1. Total Sales vs. Quota Bonus			
% of Quota Achieved	**Annual Payout per % Achievement**	**Annual Payout for Level**	**Total Annual Payout**
0%-50%	$0	$0	$0
50%-100%	$1,000	$50,000	$50,000
100%-125% and beyond	$2,000	$50,000	$100,000

2. Variable-Margin Growth Multiplier	
Achievement	**Multiplier**
<1%-1.5%	0.90
1.5%-2.0%	1.00
>2%	1.25

Payout Illustrations

- 100% of Total Sales vs. Quota is achieved
- Variable Margin has grown 0.5%
- Payout is $45,000 (the Total Sales vs. Quota incentive is multiplied by .9 since Variable-Margin growth was less than 1.5%)

- 100% of Total Sales vs. Quota is achieved
- Variable Margin has grown 2.5%
- Payout is $62,500 (the Total Sales vs. Quota incentive is multiplied by 1.25 since Variable-Margin growth was greater than 2%)

Because of the multiplier calculation, the upside leverage potential on the primary measure (i.e., total sales) must be reduced to fund the upside leverage opportunity on the multiplier component (i.e., variable-margin growth). If that is not done, excellence performance on both measures would produce a total upside-leverage payout greater than the defined leverage multiple for the plan. The process used to derive the excellence multiplier rate and maintain the desired total leverage multiple is shown here using the example incentive plan numbers from Figure 5-3:

- **Step 1:** Reduce the upside leverage on the primary component to fund upside on the multiplier. The upside leverage multiple for the primary incentive component is reduced from 2.5 to 2, producing a total upside leverage on this component of $100,000 at excellence ($50,000 x 2). The leverage on the primary component could be reduced more or less than this amount depending on how much upside "lift" is desired on the multiplier component.
- **Step 2:** Calculate how much upside leverage is remaining for the multiplier component to deliver, as follows:

Total Combined Upside at Excellence $125,000	–	Upside Leverage from Primary Component $100,000	=	Upside Leverage Remaining for Multiplier Component $25,000

- **Step 3:** Calculate the resulting excellence multiplier rate, as follows:

Upside Leverage Remaining for Multiplier Component $25,000	÷	Upside Leverage from Primary Component $100,000	+	1	=	Excellence Multiplier Rate 1.25

The reduced leverage on the primary component combined with the excellence multiplier rate results in a total incentive payout for excellence performance on both measures of $125,000 ($100,000 x 1.25 multiplier rate).

Matrices

A matrix is the most rigorous approach to relating performance in two areas. Achievement of one measure is mathematically associated with the achievement of another to determine payout. When a matrix is used, the two measures each should have a weight to construct the matrix. However, no payout is calculated based on the achievement of either measure exclusively.

As illustrated in Figure 5-4, the weights for variable margin and total sales are equal, so the values in the upper left and lower right corners of the matrix are equal. These values are lower than the value in the center cell of the matrix—

Figure 5-4
Matrix

Annual Compensation	Mix	
Annual Base Salary	50%	$50,000
Target Incentive	50%	$50,000
Target Cash Compensation	**100%**	**$100,000**
Leverage Multiple	2.50	$125,000

Quota	
Total Sales:	$5,000,000
Variable-Margin Growth:	2.0%

Performance Measures & Weights	
Measure	**Weight**
Total Sales vs. Quota	50%
Variable Margin Growth	50%
Total Value at Target	**100%**

1. Variable Margin and Total Sales vs. Quota Bonus Matrix

Variable-Margin Achievement	Payout as Percent of Target Incentive		
125.0% +	75.0%	128.6%	250.0%
100.0%-124.9%	46.4%	100.0%	128.6%
75.0%-99.9%	25.0%	46.4%	75.0%
	50.0%-99.9%	100.0%-149.9%	150.0%+
	Total Sales-Quota Achievement		

Variable-Margin Achievement	Payout Values		
125.0% +	$37,500	$64,300	$125,000
100.0%-124.9%	$23,200	$50,000	$64,300
75.0%-99.9%	$12,500	$23,200	$37,500
	50.0%-99.9%	100.0%-149.9%	150.0%+
	Total Sales Quota Achievement		

the cell that reflects target performance on both measures. The diminishing value of the incentive rate off of the center, or target performance, cell reinforces the message of the matrix to improve performance on both measures simultaneously. The performance range for each measure is different; however, threshold achievement is required for both before payout is available. Likewise, excellence performance is required on both before the maximum payout is earned. Just as with a step bonus, the bonus matrix shown here is inherently capped at excellence.

Special Incentive Illustrations

Beyond the combination commission-bonus plan and the various linked incentive techniques, there are several additional incentive formulas designed to fit special circumstances. Many of these special incentive illustrations can be used in conjunction with a combination commission-bonus plan or by using one of the linked techniques described earlier.

Adjusted-Value Plans

In an adjusted-value plan, the value of the primary performance measure (e.g., revenue, gross profit or unit volume) relative to the calculation for incentive payout (e.g., quota credit) is adjusted up or down on the basis of a secondary measure or variable, such as product mix or account type, to reflect strategic priorities (e.g., profitability or market positioning). Figure 5-5a illustrates an adjusted-value plan in which revenue volume, paid in the form of an interpolated or rate-per-point bonus, is the primary measure, and product mix is the second variable (i.e., it is not a separate plan component, but is critical to business success).

Figure 5-5a
Adjusted-Value Plan Based on Product Mix

Product-Specific Revenue Volume x

Value-Adjustment Table

Product Category	Adjustment Factor
Product A	1.30
Product B	1.15
Product C	1.00
Product D	0.70

The adjusted value of the volume for each product is used in the calculation of the total percent of quota achieved. For example, Product A volume x 1.3 = the total adjusted value used in the total quota-achievement calculation.

Monthly Revenue Bonus Schedule

Value-Adjusted Percent of Quota Achieved	Percent of Target Bonus Earned Each Level	Bonus Rate (Percent of target bonus per percent quota achieved)
60.0%-80.0%	40%	2.0%
80.1%-100.0%	60%	3.0%
100.1%-150.0%	200%	4.0%

In this example, certain products get credited toward quota achievement at a premium, while others are credited at a discount from their actual monetary value. The adjusted-value plan is unlike the linked approaches described earlier in that performance on one measure at the expense of the other is not inherently penalized. For example, in the illustration in Figure 5-5a, an exclusive focus on Product D, which gets only 70 percent credit toward quota achievement, still could produce a bonus payout well into the excellence incentive earnings range.

The adjusted-value plan approach also can be used with a commission form of incentive. One example is provided in Chapter 3: Figure 3-8 illustrates an adjusted rate commission. Figure 5-5b provides a second illustration using a commission formula. In this example, revenue volume is the primary measure paid in the form of a variable-rate commission, and account mix is the secondary variable that provides the basis for the value adjustment. In this example, revenue from new accounts and the largest existing "A" accounts is credited at a premium, while revenue from the smallest "C" accounts is discounted.

Figure 5-5b

Adjusted-Value Plan Based on Account Type

Account-Specific Revenue Volume x

Value-Adjustment Table	
Product Category	Adjustment Factor
New Accounts	1.30
Existing Accounts A	1.15
Existing Accounts B	1.00
Existing Accounts C	0.70

The adjusted value of the volume for each type of account is used in the calculation of the total adjusted-revenue volume achieved. For example, New Accounts volume x 1.3 = the total adjusted value used in the total volume-achievement calculation.

Monthly Revenue Commission Schedule

Total Adjusted-Revenue Volume ($000)	Incremental Commission Rate (Percent of revenue on each tier)
$200.0-$300.0	2.0%
$300.1-$400.0	3.0%
$400.1+	4.0%

Determining the Adjustment Factors

In designing an adjusted-value plan, the adjustment factors for each variable of the secondary measure must be modeled in the context of:

- The strategic value of each variable
- The anticipated volume
- The desired amount of incentive to be paid
- The projected effective (or base) commission rate, calculated as:

$$\frac{\text{Total Projected Cost of Incentive Compensation}}{\text{Total Projected (nonvalue-adjusted) Revenue}} = \text{Projected Effective (Base) Commission Rate}$$

- The difference between the various adjustment factors that must be significant enough to reinforce the intended selling priorities and force the desired trade-off decisions on the part of the salesperson.

New-Account Bonus

In a selling environment in which management seeks to motivate the salesforce to acquire new business, a new-account bonus can be employed to reward the acquisition of targeted new accounts. For the new-account bonus, either a binary or step bonus approach can be used.

Binary Approach

As discussed in Chapter 4, the binary approach acts as an on-off switch. On the basis of performance against the defined new-account measure, the bonus is either earned or it is not. Figure 5-6 illustrates a new-account bonus using a binary bonus approach.

In this case, the seller must acquire at least six new accounts from the target account list to qualify for the bonus. For performance of five or fewer new accounts, no bonus is earned. To employ the binary bonus approach, one must determine the minimum performance level required to earn the bonus, as well as the target bonus amount to pay for achieving the goal. Because the bonus is binary, there are only two levels in the performance range: target (which essentially is the same as threshold in this case) and below target. For cost-modeling purposes, build in assumptions for the percentage of the salesforce expected to achieve the stated target goal. This likely will be a much lower percentage than the 90-percent guideline cited in Chapter 2 for achieving threshold.

Step Approach

Figure 5-7 on page 82 illustrates the new-account bonus using a step bonus

Figure 5-6
New-Account Bonus: Binary

Annual Compensation		
	Mix	
Annual Base Salary	70%	$63,000
Target Incentive	30%	$27,000
Target Cash Compensation	**100%**	**$90,000**

Quota	
Total Sales	$1,000,000

Performance Measures & Weights			
Measure	**Weight**	**Target**	**Incentive Formula**
Total Sales vs. Quota	80%	$21,600	Commission
New Accounts	20%	$5,400	Binary Bonus
Total Value at Target	**100%**	**$27,000**	

1. Total Sales vs. Quota Commission		
Performance Range	**Total Sales**	**Commission Rate (% of Revenue)**
Up to Target	$0-$1,000,000	2.2%
Above Target	$1,000,001 and beyond	4.3%

2. New-Accounts Bonus		
Number of New Accounts Signed from the Target List	**Performance Range**	**Bonus Amount**
0-5	Below Target	$0
6+	Target+	$5,400

approach. Here, the full performance range, from threshold to target to excellence, is defined. As discussed in Chapter 4, the bonus is paid in step-rate increments as performance progresses along the range. As is the case in the binary bonus approach illustrated in Figure 5-6, the same target bonus of $5,400 is earned for target performance. However, with the step-rate approach, the bonus varies above and below the target amount with above and below goal performance, respectively.

New-Product Launch Bonus or Commission

In an environment in which frequent new products are launched or where a single, highly anticipated and strategically important new product is launched, management may seek to direct salesforce attention to the new-product activity for a defined period of time that coincides with the launch. In such cases, a new-product launch bonus or commission can be employed.

Figure 5-7

New-Account Bonus: Step

Annual Compensation		
	Mix	
Annual Base Salary	70%	$63,000
Target Incentive	30%	$27,000
Target Cash Compensation	**100%**	**$90,000**

Quota	
Total Sales	$1,000,000

Performance Measures & Weights			
Measure	**Weight**	**Target**	**Incentive Formula**
Total Sales vs. Quota	80%	$21,600	Commission
New Accounts	20%	$5,400	Step Bonus
Total Value at Target	**100%**	**$27,000**	

1. Total Sales vs. Quota Commission

Performance Range	Total Sales	Commission Rate (% of Revenue)
Up to Target	$0-$1,000,000	2.2%
Above Target	$1,000,001 and beyond	4.3%

2. New-Accounts Bonus

Number of New Accounts Signed from the Target List	Performance Range	Bonus Amount
0-1	< Threshold	$0
2-3	Threshold	$1,350
4-5		$2,700
6-7	Target	$5,400
8-9		$8,100
10+	Excellence	$10,800

Because the specific timing of a new-product launch can be highly variable and, at times, difficult to predict, it often is difficult to build into the core sales-incentive plan a constant incentive component that regularly measures and rewards for new-product sales results. As such, a new-product launch incentive often is designed in advance, but kept "on the shelf" and inactivated until the product launch takes place. Therefore, these types of incentives are frequently "out of plan" or additional incentive opportunities, such as a contest or SPIFF. The process for determining the value of the payout per salesperson is the same process used to determine a commission rate or bonus payout rate; however, the budget is established outside of the target incentive budget.

A new-product launch incentive can be devised in the form of a bonus or commission. Figure 5-8 illustrates a new-product launch bonus. Because this is a bonus, it requires the definition of an explicit quota or goal for the new-product volume. Such a quota may or may not be easy to establish accurately. A bonus may be appropriate where the demand for the new product is relatively easy to predict, such as with a simple extension of a well-known and proven product that is sold in a known market.

Figure 5-8

New Product Launch Bonus

90-Day New-Product Launch Bonus Schedule		
90-Day Percent of New-Product Quota Achieved	Percent of Target Bonus Earned Each Level	Bonus Level (Percent of target bonus per percent quota achieved)
0.0%-50.0%	40%	0.8%
50.1%-100.0%	60%	1.2%
100.1%-150.0%	200%	4.0%

Conversely, if the new product represents a new and untested product category, or is sold into a new and unknown market, the task of setting realistic quotas may be impossible. In such cases, the new-product launch incentive should be delivered in the form of a commission. Figure 5-9 illustrates a new-product launch commission in which the rate varies with new-product revenue volume, but is not governed on the basis of quota attainment.

Figure 5-9

New-Product Launch Commission

90-Day New-Product Launch Commission Schedule	
90-Day New-Product Revenue Volume ($000)	Incremental Commission Rate (Percent of revenue on each tier)
$0.0-$25.0	8%
$25.1-$50.0	12%
$50.1+	15%

In addition to the decision about the type of incentive formula to use, there are other important considerations when structuring a new-product launch incentive:

- **Timing**. The new-product launch incentive should start with the launch of the product (or when preselling efforts are expected to begin) and continue for a defined term corresponding with the amount of time required to achieve the desired initial product placement in the market. After the incentive term expires, the ongoing volume from the new product is paid through the core incentive plan.

- **Incentive value.** It is important to establish an appropriate monetary value for the new-product launch incentive. It must be enough to get the sales-force's attention, but not so much that it overshadows the core sales-incentive plan. The latter is of particular concern in environments characterized by frequent new-product launches. If frequent launch incentives pay too much relative to the incentive opportunity in the core plan, it may elicit "sandbagging," where salespeople simply coast along for the brief period until the next new-product incentive is introduced, where they perceive the "real money" is to be earned. Chapters 3 and 8 of *Sales Compensation Essentials* provides additional discussion on using SPIFFs and contests.
- **Post-Launch Plan Adjustments.** After the product launch incentive period ends and payment for ongoing new-product volume reverts to the core plan, it is important to adjust quotas or incentive formulas accordingly to account for the addition of the new-product volume. Absent such an adjustment, over-payment of incentive is likely.
- **Budgeting for the incentive.** Budgeting for the product-launch incentive is based on whether the incentive is "at-risk" and, thus, considered part of the target incentive, or whether it is considered an "add-on" item in addition to the target incentive.

Sales Incentive Pay Linked to Balanced Scorecard (BSC)

BSC is a measurement framework that companies use to define strategic goals at every level of the organization and align measures to each goal so that managers can take improvement action as required. Developed in 1992 by Harvard Business School professors David Norton and Robert Kaplan, BSC has steadily grown in usage and importance.[1] In recent years, there has been an interest in applying BSC concepts and principles to the design of sales incentive plans. This often is the case in companies where BSC already is used for other functions, and the sales organization's incentive plans would benefit from the same approach because it would establish consistency across plans.

When to Use a BSC for the Sales Incentive Compensation Plan

This approach should be considered as an alternative to other "linked" designs

(1) "The Balanced Scorecard: Translating Strategy into Action," by Robert S. Kaplan and David P. Norton (*Harvard Business School Press*, September 1996.)

(e.g., a hurdle, multiplier and/or matrix, as previously described). The principal benefit of a BSC incentive design is that it integrates multiple measures of performance with a single results score that can be related to a payout amount. Thus, it minimizes (but does not eliminate) visible formula complexity. The single results score ensures that payout is perceived as significant (compared to the practice of a linked design using a hurdle or multiplier that may result in two or three separate payouts) and provides an opportunity to link more than two measures of performance (the limitation of a matrix). Use of a BSC approach to sales incentive pay should be considered when:

- Dissimilar performance measures are used, but there is a benefit to linking performance across those measures and rewarding results through a single performance score
- There is wide variability in performance ranges.

How to Calculate Sales Incentive Pay Using BSC

Figure 5-10a provides an illustration of a BSC incentive plan for a technical sales representative position. This sales specialist role provides technical support to account managers who are responsible for selling to and managing business with a defined set of accounts. To create a BSC incentive plan for this position, three steps are involved:

- **Step 1: Establish the Performance Scorecard.** This requires identifying the appropriate performance measures and assigning appropriate incentive

Figure 5-10a
Balanced Scorecard Illustration

Technical Sales Representative Plan	Mix		
Annual Base Salary	91%	$50,000	
Target Incentive	9%	$5,000	10% of Base Salary
Target Cash Compensation	**100%**	**$55,000**	
Leverage Multiple	**1.5**	**$7,500**	

Performance Scorecard						
Measure	**Weight**	**Achievement Level**				
Total Business Unit Dollars vs. Target	40%	85%	92.5%	100%	107.5%	115%
Business Unit Emphasis Product Dollars vs. Target	35%	90%	95%	100%	105%	110%
Individual Strategic Objectives	25%	50%	-	100%	-	150%
Total Weight	**100%**	**78**	**83**	**100**	**105**	**12**
		Threshold		**Target**		**Excellence**

weights. This process and the related math are described in Chapter 2.

- **Step 2: Determine the Scorecard Points Associated with Performance Achievement Levels.** The point value associated with each achievement level is calculated using the following formula:

$$\text{Achievement Level Points} = [\text{Sum of Each Element of (Weight x Performance Level)}] \times 100$$

  Example: In Figure 5-10a, the threshold point value is calculated as follows:

$$\text{Threshold Performance} = [(.40 \times .85) + (.35 \times .90) + (.25 \times .50)] \times 100$$
$$= [(.34) + (.315) + (.125)] \times 100 = 78 \text{ points}$$

  The same calculation is applied to all other achievement levels in the performance scorecard table.

- **Step 3: Calculate the Incentive Payout Table.** The payout table can be developed from three to five tiers. It three tiers are used, then each tier is bounded by the defined performance levels (e.g., threshold, target and excellence). If five tiers are used, then each intervening tier is calculated based on the difference between the preceding and succeeding tier. Assuming that the tiers are numbered one, two, three, four and five, then the initial calculations to determine each tier are:
  - Tier 1 boundaries:
    - Zero
    - Threshold
  - Tier 2 boundaries:
    - Threshold + 1
    - [(Target – Threshold) / 2] + Threshold
  - Tier 3 boundaries:
    - [({Target – Threshold} / 2) + Threshold] + 1
    - Target
  - Tier 4 boundaries:
    - Target + 1
    - [(Excellence – Target) / 2] + Target
  - Tier 5 boundaries:
    - [({Excellence – Target} / 2) + Target] + 1
    - Excellence

Figure 5-10b provides an illustrative incentive payout table and incentive payout calculation.

Figure 5-10b

Calculation Illustration

Incentive Payout Table			
Total Points Achieved	% of Target Incentive Compensation	Payout (% of Salary)	Annual Payout (Dollars)
0-77	0%	0.0%	$0
78-89	50%	5.0%	$2,500
90-100	100%	10.0%	$5,000
101-111	125%	12.5%	$6,250
112-122	150%	15.0%	$7,500

Payout Calculator: Annual Amount			
Measure	**Achievement**	**Points**	**Annual Payout**
Total BU Dollars vs. Target	100%	40.0	
BU Emphasis Product Dollars vs. Target	95%	33.25	
Individual Strategic Objectives	100%	25.0	
Total Points		**98.25**	**$5,000**

Once these initial boundaries are established for each tier, they may be adjusted based on financial viability. For example, if the company has determined that target pay should not be available until at least 95 points are achieved based on financial modeling, then tiers two and three would be adjusted to reflect that decision.

Key Sales Objectives

A key sales objectives (KSO) bonus is an MBO-type of incentive formula, but for use with measurable and quantifiable performance goals. While the KSOs may be milestones or process oriented, taking this approach reduces the discretionary bent of many MBO bonuses. For certain roles in a complex selling environment, the typical volume (e.g., revenue) and quality (e.g., product mix) performance measures may not fully reflect the strategic essence of the role. In these instances, management may need the flexibility to set account-specific goals that may be unique from one salesperson to the next. Figure 5-11 on page 88 illustrates an example KSO bonus based on three measures.

There are several important considerations in establishing a KSO bonus, including:

- **Number of Measures.** As discussed in Chapter 2, the number of performance measures should be limited to as few as possible to ensure clarity of focus. The same is true for KSO measures. This is particularly important given that the KSO component is typically a secondary or tertiary measure in the sales compensation plan. Because KSOs typically represent no more than 25

Figure 5-11
Key Sales Objectives Bonus

KSO	Weight	Target Quarterly Bonus	Performance Range Percent of Target Bonus Earned: Below Threshold 0%	Threshold 50%	Target 100%	Excellence 150%	Illustrative Bonus Payout
1	50%	$2,500				X	$3,750 $2,500x150%
2	30%	$1,500			X		$1,500 $1,500x100%
3	20%	$1,000		X			$500 $1,000x50%
Total	100%	$5,000					$5,750

Illustrative KSO Measures	Performance Range / Definition: Threshold	Target	Excellence
1. Identify new opportunities to sell Product A in targeted accounts.	Orders placed in two accounts	Orders placed in four accounts	Orders placed in six or more accounts
2. Displace competition to secure a long-term service contract.	Service contract secured in one account	Service contract secured in two accounts	Service contract secured in four or more accounts
3. Average customer-satisfaction survey ratings results.	Rating of 3.0	Rating of 3.75	Rating of 4.5 or better

percent of the target incentive compensation opportunity, limiting the number of KSOs makes attainment of each financially meaningful.

- **Types of Measures.** KSO measures must be measurable and quantifiable, requiring as little management judgment as possible. As such, management must have the ability to set realistic goals for each measure. The KSO performance range should be nonbinary (i.e., using the full performance range, from threshold to excellence). If necessary, the measures can change each performance period depending on seasonal factors or changing market conditions.
- **Weighting of Each Measure.** Also discussed in Chapter 2, the KSO measures must be weighted to reflect their relative priority, just as the KSO component itself must be weighted relative to other incentive plan components or measures. The sum of the KSO measure weights must equal 100 percent.
- **Length of Performance Period.** The length of the performance period and the resulting payout frequency for the KSO bonus must be established in the context of the expected time horizon required to achieve the various KSO measures. For example, if the sales cycle for a particular KSO measure is at least nine months, then incorporating that measure into a quarterly KSO bonus will result in missed earnings opportunities and disgruntled salespeople.
- **KSO Administration.** Properly managing a KSO bonus clearly is more time

consuming for sales management staff. This largely is due to the challenge of selecting performance measures that may differ by salesperson and the differentiated goal-setting process that comes with that. In addition, because measures and goals often are unique by sales representative, ongoing performance tracking, evaluation and reporting may be manual in nature on the part of the sales management team. Therefore, it is critical to first confirm that including a KSO component is necessary. Then guidelines must be established, including:

- A limited "menu" of approved and relevant KSO performance measures from which sales managers can choose
- Using only measures for which there are systems that can track and measure performance
- Appropriate goal setting, performance evaluation and reporting processes.

Fast-Start Incentives

All companies are interested in getting off to a fast start to achieve a new year's business goals. This is particularly true in businesses that experience either seasonality in consumer buying (e.g., Q2 and Q3 are the strongest quarters because the product is most frequently used during the summer months) or cyclicality in business buying (e.g., Q4 is the strongest quarter because corporate buyers want to spend their budget before year-end). In an effort to offset this variability in buying and move sales forward, management uses a "fast-start" incentive element in the sales compensation plan. The most common fast-start practice is to apply a multiplier to incentive compensation earned in the first quarter when actual performance meets or exceeds target performance. Figure 5-12 illustrates a fast-start incentive plan component of a sales compensation plan.

As indicated in Figure 5-12, the calculation of a fast-start bonus requires two variables: the amount of incentive earned under the plan formula and the "multiplier"—the factor used to "plus up" the base amount of incentive earned when fast-start perform-

Figure 5-12

Fast-Start Incentive

Performance Range	Fast Incentive Award:
If actual performance is...	**IC defined by formula in plan (X) times multiplier**
Below threshold	1
Greater than threshold but less than target performance	1
Target or greater, but less than excellence performance	120% times X
Excellence performance or greater	140% times X

ance is achieved. Typically, the first-quarter quota or sales goal is the most challenging objective to achieve, particularly in businesses in which historical sales are 20 percent or less of total volume. Thus, if a salesperson meets or exceeds the first quarter sales quota, premium incentive compensation (i.e., the target incentive pay in addition to a "plus up" award reflected by size of the multiplier) is paid for that achievement.

The reason a "multiplier" is preferred to, for example, a fixed-dollar bonus is that the magnitude of additional incentive earned is tied to how good a job a salesperson does relative to achieving/exceeding expected performance. How large the fast-start bonus should be (i.e., the size of the multiplier) is largely a judgment based on the financial value of the business that has been "pulled forward." However, best practice suggests that, to have a motivational impact, the fast-start bonus should provide an additional incentive award in the range of 20 percent to 25 percent of the target award. Thus, in Figure 5-12, the actual incentive earned is multiplied by 120 percent for performance that is target or greater, but less than excellence performance. Performance at excellence or greater is rewarded at two times the first-tier rate (20 percent x 2 = 40 percent, or 140 percent of the actual earned incentive).

The funds for a fast-start bonus typically are carved out of the upside incentive opportunity. For example, if the target incentive opportunity is $40,000, and the upside (i.e., leverage) is two times, or $80,000, then the actual upside in the incentive formula design would be reduced by an amount equal to the second-tier multiplier. In this example, the excellence at $80,000 would result in the following opportunities at excellence for each quarter:

$$\left(\frac{\$80{,}000}{4.4}\right) \times 1.4 = \$25{,}455 \text{ (Q1 fast-start incentive at excellence)}$$

$$\left(\frac{\$80{,}000}{4.4}\right) \times 3 = \$54{,}545 \text{ (Balance of upside opportunity or \$18,182 per quarter at excellence for Q2, Q3, Q4)}$$

In this calculation, 4.4 represents the value of the incentive allocated across the four quarters, with a 40 percent (0.4) premium attached to Q1.

Consistency Bonus

To motivate and reward consistent achievement of performance goals over a defined time period, management may include a consistency bonus opportunity in the sales compensation plan. This feature is most common in the sales compensation plans of startup companies with rapid growth expectations where consistent, quarterly performance achievement is important to attracting venture capital or equity market funds. Consistency bonuses also are used in the sales compensation plans of publicly traded companies where consistent attainment of quarterly growth is critical to maintaining a high stock price. Thus, rewarding the salesforce for contributing to consistent results is an important design consideration.

A consistency bonus is associated with a performance measure. Essentially, that performance measure is the one for which consistent results is the key indicator of business success. This type of bonus may be considered a part of the target incentive or the upside, based on the degree to which quarter-to-quarter achievement of goal is considered stretch performance.

If consistency is considered target performance, then a consistency bonus is part of the target incentive. In this case, consistency is given a weight, and the formula used to calculate payout can be a true bonus or a multiplier. Figure 5-13a provides an example of a consistency bonus. This bonus is based on a target of $20,000 for quarterly consistency. The payout accelerates so that each quarter is worth more than Q1 multiplied by the number of quarters.

Figure 5-13a
Quarterly Consistency Bonus (Target)

Number of Quarters	Payout
1	$1,500
2	$4,500
3	$6,000
4	$8,000

If quarter-to-quarter consistency is considered a stretch, then the consistency bonus is funded through the leverage or upside available in the plan. Figure 5-13b provides an example of this approach. Here, the core plan component is a commission on revenue, and the consistency bonus is delivered in the form of a multiplier. The consistency bonus is in addition to the earned incentive; for this bonus the calculation is cumulative and begins with the second quarter if the first and second quarter targets are achieved. The actual earned incentive for the first quarter plus the actual earned incentive for the second quarter is multiplied by 105 percent. That is, an additional 5 percent is earned midyear.

Figure 5-13b
Quarterly Consistency Bonus (Upside)

Consecutive Achievement	Multiplier
Q2	105%
Q3	110%
Q4	115%

Linearity Incentives

Similar to the consistency bonus that is used to reward for consistent performance *across* performance periods, a linearity incentive is used to reward for smooth and consistent performance attainment over the months *within* the performance period, most often a quarter. The linearity incentive is used to counter the "hockey stick" phenomenon, where business tends to be back-end loaded within a given quarter, thus creating operational challenges in the manufacture and/or delivery of a high volume of product over a compressed time frame. In such a case, management may seek to pull business into the first and second months of the quarter.

For example, consider the company where two-thirds of its quarterly business comes in the last month of the quarter, and late within the third month, at that. A linearity incentive may be advised to pay more incentive for realizing a greater percentage of the quarterly quota in months one and two. Figure 5-14a illustrates an example of a quarterly linearity bonus as a secondary measure that complements the primary revenue measure.

Figure 5-14a

Quarterly Linearity Bonus

Performance Range	Month 2 QTD % of Quarterly Quota Achieved	Bonus Rate (% of Target Bonus)
< Threshold	0.0%-54.9%	0%
Threshold	55.0%-59.9%	25%
	60.0%-66.6%	60%
Target	66.7%-74.9%	100%
	75.0%-84.9%	150%
Excellence	85.0% +	200%

In this example, the seller is encouraged to generate a greater percentage of the quarterly quota in months one and two combined. The linearity bonus depicted in Figure 5-14a is an unlinked or stand-alone bonus intended to complement the primary volume measure. As this example illustrates, the linearity incentive typically is funded as a part of the target incentive compensation structure.

In addition to separate, unlinked incentive components, the linearity incentive can be structured using the linked techniques described earlier in this chapter. Figure 5-14b illustrates a linearity incentive in the form of a linked multiplier.

As shown, the performance measure (the percentage of the quarterly quota achieved in months one and two) remains the same as in the unlinked quarterly linearity bonus example. However, the multiplier links the linearity payout to

Figure 5-14b

Quarterly Linearity Multiplier

Performance Range	Month 2 QTD % of Quarterly Quota Achieved	Multiplier (% of Quarterly Bonus Earnings)
< Threshold	0.0%-54.9%	-15.0%
Threshold	55.0%-59.9%	10.0%
	60.0%-66.6%	17.5%
Target	66.7%-74.9%	25.0%
	75.0%-84.9%	30.0%
Excellence	85.0% +	35.0%

the primary volume measure, further reinforcing the priorities of:

- Achieve and exceed quota, and
- Achieve the quarterly quota in a balanced fashion.

Notice also that for below-threshold performance, the multiplier reduces the value of the bonus earned on the primary component, further reinforcing the desired behavior.

Lastly, Figure 5-15 illustrates a monthly linearity bonus that tracks quota attainment in months one and two separately. As shown in this example, the target bonus amount in months one and two is the same, at $1,000. However, the upside bonus opportunity increases in month two, reflecting the desire to avoid the month three hockey stick.

Figure 5-15

Monthly Linearity Bonus

Month 1 Linearity Bonus

Performance Range	Month 1 QTD % of Quarterly Quota Achieved	Month 1 Bonus
< Threshold	0.0%-24.9%	$0
Threshold	25.0%-29.9%	$250
	30.0%-33.2%	$500
Target	33.3%-35.9%	$1,000
	36.0%-39.9%	$1,500
Excellence	40.0% +	$2,000

Month 2 Linearity Bonus

Performance Range	Month 2 QTD % of Quarterly Quota Achieved	Month 2 Bonus
< Threshold	0.0%-54.9%	$0
Threshold	55.0%-59.9%	$250
	60.0%-66.6%	$500
Target	66.7%-74.9%	$1,000
	75.0%-84.9%	$2,000
Excellence	85.0% +	$3,000

Summing Up

Balancing the imperatives of plan relevance and plan complexity is an ever-present challenge in the sales compensation design process. Above all, a sales incentive plan must be relevant to the role and reflective of the company's business objectives and go-to-market strategy. If, however, a sales incentive plan is perceived as overly complex, its desired motivational impact will be lost as salespeople begin to tune out. In fact, the use of any of the advanced incentive techniques described here in Chapter 5 is likely to increase the complexity of a sales compensation plan. The question is whether the nature of the role and the context of the selling environment warrant the advanced incentive technique and make the increased complexity acceptable or even necessary.

"Key Sales Incentive Plan Practices," recent primary research conducted by WorldatWork, confirms the importance of balancing relevance and complexity, specifically pointing to the desire to avoid overly complex plans. In a survey of its member base on sales incentive compensation practices, 22.3 percent of respondents indicated the primary reason for plan change was to reduce incentive plan complexity. Even more respondents (44 percent) indicated that the primary driver for plan change was to improve alignment with the business strategy.

Clearly, achieving the desired balance in a sales compensation plan is not an easy task. However, this challenge reinforces the need to have the right cross-functional team involved in the sales compensation design process to generate the variety of perspectives that will result in considered and appropriate design decisions.

About the Authors

Jerome ("Jerry") A. Colletti is Managing Partner, Colletti-Fiss, LLC, a management-consulting firm with headquarters in Scottsdale, Ariz., that helps management make decisions about programs that increase sales results. Colletti-Fiss focuses on three areas of sales effectiveness: jobs design and organization structure, performance management programs and sales compensation plans. Colletti and his associates help *Fortune* 500 companies use these programs effectively so they can grow profitably, serve customers wisely and reward employees appropriately for achieving business objectives on a worldwide basis.

Colletti is the author of more than 100 publications and frequently is quoted in leading business publications and journals, including *The Wall Street Journal* and *Harvard Business Review*. His most recent article for the *Harvard Business Review*, co-authored by Mary Fiss, "The Ultimately Accountable Job: Leading Today's Sales Organization," appeared in the July/August 2006 issue. His most recent book, *Sales Compensation Essentials: A Field Guide for the HR Professional*, co-authored with Mary Fiss, Ted Briggs and Scott Sands, was published by WorldatWork in March 2006. The second edition of his book *Compensating New Sales Roles: How to Design Rewards that Work in Today's Selling Environment*, also co-authored by Mary Fiss, was published by AMACOM Books in June 2001.

He has been a WorldatWork course instructor for "C5: Elements of Sales Compensation" since 1979. In 2004, he co-authored "Sales Compensation for Complex Selling Models," another WorldatWork course.

Mary S. Fiss is a Partner in the management consulting firm Colletti-Fiss, LLC. She has extensive experience in the development and implementation of sales compensation plans, variable pay plans for teams, reward and recognition, professional development and performance management programs. Fiss works with clients on issues and challenges related to increasing salesforce productivity through the effective use of compensation and management education programs.

She frequently is quoted in popular business publications and is the author of more than 30 articles, book chapters and books. She is a co-author of *Sales Compensation Essentials: A Field Guide for the HR Professional* with Jerry Colletti, Ted Briggs and Scott Sands, published by WorldatWork in March 2006. With Jerry Colletti, Fiss wrote "Designing Sales Incentive Pay for Competitive Advantage," which appeared in Chapter 3 in *Incentive Pay: Creating a Competitive Advantage*, published by WorldatWork in 2007. She co-authored the second edition of *Compensating New Sales Roles: How to Design Rewards that Work in Today's Selling Environment* with Jerry Colletti, published by AMACOM Books in June 2001.

J. Mark Davis is Managing Principal of Valitus Group, Inc., an Orange County, Calif.-based management consulting firm specializing in improving salesforce effectiveness through solutions firmly grounded in a client organization's business objectives.

A management consultant since 1990, Davis has extensive experience working with *Fortune* 500 to midmarket companies on a global scale. His client work focuses on the design and implementation of sales compensation plans that align sales resources with company objectives to produce meaningful results.

Davis is a contributing author of *The Sales Compensation Handbook*, Second Edition, published by AMACOM in 1998, and a frequent speaker on the topic of salesforce compensation. He is a WorldatWork faculty member, teaching "Sales Compensation for Complex Selling Models," and is regularly quoted in many leading business publications, including *BusinessWeek*, *USA Today*, *Selling Power*, *Sales & Marketing Management* and *HR Executive*.

Davis earned a B.S.B.A., cum laude, from Northern Arizona University, and an M.B.A. with a concentration in marketing from the Cox School of Business at Southern Methodist University.